Living the Gospel as a Way of Life

Building a Spiritual Culture

by James R. Jones

with Gabriel Meyer

A City of the Lord Publication

Phoenix Los Angeles San Diego Monterey

Publisher: City of the Lord
              711 W. University
              Tempe, Arizona 85282
              (480) 968-5990
              www.cityofthelord.org

City of the Lord is officially established as a Private Association of the Christian Faithful and Private Juridic Person of Diocesan Right by Bishop Thomas J. Olmsted, May 8th, 2012. City of the Lord is also a founding member of the Catholic Fraternity, a private association of the Catholic faithful, established in the Vatican by Saint John Paul on November 30, 1990.

Printed in the United States of America

Living the Gospel as a Way of Life: Building a Spiritual Culture

Written by James R. Jones with Gabriel Meyer

Cover Artist: Mary V. McGuire

ISBN-10:0991532708

ISBN-13:978-0-9915327-0-4

City of the Lord

A Catholic Charismatic Covenant Community
Phoenix • LosAngeles • SanDiego • MontereyBay

With Gratitude

It is with heartfelt gratitude that we dedicate this book to the men and women who, in the beginning days of the charismatic renewal, were touched on the shoulder by Jesus who said, "Come and follow Me." As the Apostles of old, they left the diverse occupations that consumed their lives and, in the power of the Holy Spirit, followed Jesus with all their resources of mind, body and spirit, and placed their many gifts at the foot of the Cross.

These courageous men and women, over the course of a few years, met one another and found companions who shared the same vison to build a community of people dedicated to placing our lives as brothers and sisters under the reign of the Lord Jesus to love and serve God and one another with our whole lives and to follow His plan wherever it may lead.

This group of men and women, who caught the vision of community in the early '70s, came together as founders to build one community called City of the Lord out of four separate locations in the western United States. It is a living testimony to the Lord's incredible love for us that we are still together as brothers and sisters after 40 years of trial, tribulations and ultimate joy of serving our Lord Jesus in His unfolding plan.

We extend a very special "thank you" to Dan Sauer, Bob Carmody, Martin Nagy and Jim Hyde for your constant encouragement, your support and your expert guidance. This book would never have been written without you.

Foreword

It's all about the Love. In 2002 my wife, Halyna, and I responded to an invitation to spend a year with the community called City of the Lord in Tempe, AZ. The invitation was simple but moving: "You two seem tired, burnt out. Come spend the coming year with us and we will love you back to life." How often does one get an invitation like that? What is more astounding is that the members of this community were true to their word. What is behind a love that is so powerful? Solid formation, which is all too rare in today's confused and confusing world. In *Living the Gospel as a Way of Life: Building a Spiritual Culture*, Jim Jones and Gabriel Meyer have given us a text that encompasses the formation in what the authors refer to as "the constituent elements of Christian love" that is regularly given to members of City of The Lord.

This book is a tried-and-true compendium on how to practically live the Christian life in its day-to-day reality: how to preserve right speech, how to live gratitude, how to honor others, how to be kind and reliable, how to repair relationships and live with disagreements, how to put family back at the heart of things. All of this is broken into digestible pieces. That doesn't make them easy, of course. It is easy to read this wisdom, since the style is very readable. What is hard is to live it. But that is where doing it with others makes all the difference. That is what community is all about. Deep down, isn't that what we all long for in our loneliness and alienation: people that we can commit ourselves to because we can see that they are already committed to us in an approximation of how God has committed Himself to us?

The teachings in this book are not starry-eyed pious treatises that would be off-putting to the average North American believer. Everything that the reader will find in this volume has already been realized in the daily interactions of the hundreds of members of City of the Lord, the Catholic charismatic covenant community that my wife and I have belonged to since the early 2000's. These people don't levitate. Their holiness is borne out by their determination to live for each other in the power of the Holy Spirit. They have decided to treat each other as neighbor, as brother and sister, even on the days when the other is less than lovable, which can be a lot of days!

I have spoken at various conferences in North America and abroad and to my many students at the Metropolitan Andrey Sheptytsky Institute of Eastern

Christian Studies about the astounding love that we have continually encountered in this covenant community. Many have asked me how this could be replicated elsewhere, especially in parish life. This book offers an answer to those questions. Of course, at the root of everything that is spiritually fruitful is the action of the Lord Himself. But a response must be made to the love of God. That response needs to be incarnate in the hundreds of concrete decisions of our everyday lives. This book serves as an essential guide for those decisions: a veritable manual for those who want to transform their own families and communities through practical discipleship.

Christians are to be recognizable by their love for one another. This book shows how a community can achieve that kind of love. All Catholics, whether Roman or Eastern Catholic should find these teachings practical and life-giving. I heartily endorse this book and encourage dioceses, seminaries, religious communities and parishes, as well as other intentional groupings of the faithful, to take the teachings of this book to heart and to begin to give the faithful the kind of formation that they deserve - a formation that will equip them for life in the very challenging circumstances in which Christians find themselves today. This is how it is possible for sinners to live in the Kingdom of God, even here, even now.

Andriy, sinner-priest

Rt. Rev. Mitred Protopresbyter Andriy Chirovsky, S.Th.D.

Peter and Doris Kule Professor of Eastern Christian Theology and Spirituality;
Founder and First Director, Metropolitan Andrey Sheptytsky Institute of Eastern
  Christian Studies;
Faculty of Theology, Saint Paul University, Ottawa, Canada;
Faculty of Graduate and Postdoctoral Studies, University of Ottawa (Ottawa,
  Canada);
Pastor, St. Michael Ukrainian Catholic Church, Tucson, AZ
Member, City of the Lord

September 17, 2014

Contents

Introduction

This book, *Living the Gospel as a Way of Life*, is the fruit of the experience of thousands of Catholic lay people all over the world. It is not the work of a single author nor does it reflect the perspective of a single group of people. The spiritual principles outlined in these pages have been developed, honed, tested, and lived over a period of more than forty years by people from many different backgrounds who came together in many different circumstances to seek a "life in the Spirit" and to offer the gifts God gave them to the service of the Church and the world.

But if many hands have contributed to the principles on Christian relationships presented in this workbook, the precise way they have been assembled here reflects the experience of City of the Lord, a Catholic lay community headquartered in Phoenix, Arizona, with branches in Los Angeles, San Diego, and Monterey, California.

Our community, along with dozens of similar lay associations, emerged out of the Catholic charismatic renewal in the 1970s more than 40 years ago as part of a broad impetus in charismatic prayer groups to form intentional communities. This urge to form community follows the logic of Catholic spiritual movements in the past, in which the ideals of a particular spirituality are fleshed out in communities, where those ideals can evolve into a whole way of life, into a particular witness to the Gospel.

Following a call from recent popes that Catholic charismatic communities place themselves at the service of the broader Church, we have been assessing the gifts God has given us and exploring ways to share them with fellow Catholics in parishes, religious communities, and families. Two gifts in particular continue to animate our lives:

1. the call to open our lives each day to the power of the Holy Spirit, and
2. the call to live concretely as brothers and sisters in the Lord.

We believe that these two gifts have meaning for every Catholic, not just for people living in special communities or religious associations. A life empowered by the Holy Spirit is the heritage of every Catholic by virtue of the sacraments. A life empowered by love is the very heart of the Gospel, applicable in every situation: family, parish, parish council, convent, school, workplace, and neighborhood.

What this book offers is a distillation of some of the practical wisdom the Lord has given us over the years – through much trial and error – practical teaching on how to live concretely, in the here and now, as brothers and sisters in the Lord, a short course on what might well be called the constituent elements of Christian love.

We won't attempt to give a full treatment of these topics here, just the core principles; there's much more to learn about each of these areas than we will cover in this book. But in our experience the "first things" and six "building blocks" of a spiritual culture outlined in these pages are the essential place to start. I assure you that there's nothing new or original in the topics we have chosen. You'll find little here that you, as a practicing Catholic, don't already know, at least intuitively. But I can tell you that many of these teachings, drawn from Scripture and the tradition of the Church, came to us, in our community experience, as something of a revelation as well as an ongoing challenge. It's not too much to say that the attempt to take these Christian personal relationships principles seriously, day by day, along with the abundant grace of the Holy Spirit, is what has made our community life, in the practical sense, a possibility.

Over the years, we've been heartened by the testimony of fellow Catholics, outside the community, who, through our retreats and parish training programs, have found this material as startlingly relevant and as life-giving as we have, as meaningful and helpful in their own lives and families as it has been in ours.

It's worth saying, however, that what we offer here is less a set of prescriptions than a vision : a vision of what the Christian life can look like if we open our hearts and minds to God's plan and ask the Holy Spirit to teach us how to live, a vision of the spiritual culture meant to be part and parcel of Catholic life and the foundation of the work of the New Evangelization, a vision of Catholic life. This is the important part. The practical suggestions we offer, which reflect our community experience, readers will need to apply with discernment to their own particular circumstances and to the context in which the Lord has placed them. Much here will depend on whether this book is being used in a family setting, as a guide for a parish or convent retreat, as training material for a parish council, small group or lay association, or as a source for personal reflection.

One final note: In order for any of this material to have its full effect in our lives, it will need to be seen in the context of a personal commitment to the

Lord. The art of Christian love is not a matter of mastering a few principles or adopting a few new personal habits. It is about submitting our whole lives to God. No methodology will do much for us if we're not committed to becoming step by faltering step, day by day, faculty by faculty, God's own people (1 Peter 2:9) – so that our way of life might model God's saving love and mercy to the world.

As we will stress throughout this book, the work of building Christian brotherhood and sisterhood is, from start to finish, the work of the Holy Spirit, who wishes to form in all of us, whatever our station or circumstance, the character of Jesus Himself, and to lead us onward, as Pope Saint John Paul has urged, in building a "civilization of love."

As you undertake this spiritual journey, I pray that the Lord will complete the good work He has begun in you to the honor and glory of His kingdom.

James R. Jones

Part 1
First Things

Chapter 1

The Great Commandment

God who created man out of love also calls him to love—the fundamental and innate vocation of every human being. For man is created in the image and likeness of God who is himself love.

Catechism of the Catholic Church (1604)

Everything begins and ends with love. Jesus Himself teaches this in a famous scene found in both Matthew and Luke's Gospels:

And [a lawyer] asked him a question, to test him. "Teacher, which is the great commandment in the law?" And [Jesus] said to him: "You shall love the Lord your God with all your heart, and with all your soul, and with all your mind. This is the great and first commandment. And a second is like it, you shall love your neighbor as yourself. On these two commandments depend all the law and the prophets." (Matthew 22:35-40)

And behold, a lawyer stood up to put him to the test, saying, "Teacher, what shall I do to inherit eternal life?" [Jesus] said to him, "What is written in the law? How do you read it?" And he answered, "You shall love the Lord your God with all your heart, and with all your soul, and with all your strength, and with all your mind; and your neighbor as yourself." And he said to him, "You have answered right; do this, and you will live." (Luke 10:25-28)

Love God and Love Your Neighbor

Jesus' questioners may have been attempting to embroil Him in the religious controversies of the day; but they are also asking a serious question: Out of all the welter of laws and ordinances prescribed for God's people, is there a fundamental principle that puts them all into perspective, upon which all of them depend—a ruling precept that provides a sense of definition and priority to all the choices we're called to make in our daily lives that orders, informs, and empowers the way God's people are supposed to live?

The Lord's reply, echoing the *Shema*[1], the confession at the heart of Jewish prayer, is definitive: "You shall love the Lord your God with all your heart, with all your soul, and with all your mind. This is the great and first commandment. And a second is like it, you shall love your neighbor as yourself. On these two commandments depend [or hang] all the law and the prophets."

The call to love God and neighbor, Jesus is saying, is the sum of all Scripture (the Law and the Prophets), and the totality of the life He is training His disciples to lead. As we see throughout the Gospels, the Lord's dispute with his opponents, particularly with elements of the Pharisee movement, had to do with their skewed sense of priorities, in which ritual purity laws and ascetical traditions took precedence over the overarching demands of love.

"You [Pharisees] tithe the mint, and dill, and cumin, and have neglected the weightier matters of the law—justice and mercy and faith; these you ought to have done without neglecting the others."

(Matthew 23:23)

Augustine, in his famous work *On Christian Doctrine*, reinforces this teaching by insisting that love of God and love of neighbor constitute the lens through which Christians look in order to understand and interpret the Bible, in whole or in part:

Whoever, then, thinks that he understands the Holy Scriptures, or any part of them, but puts such an interpretation upon them as does not tend to build up this two-fold love of God and our neighbor, does not yet understand them as he ought.

Augustine goes even further:

The whole temporal dispensation for our salvation...was framed by the providence of God that we might know this truth [the call to love God and neighbor] and be able to act upon it.

Nature itself, Augustine declares, and the providence that orders our lives, is arranged so that we might perceive the centrality of the love of God and neighbor in our lives, "and be able to act upon it." All the means by which we might know and have access to reality itself affirm this truth.

Notice, however, that the Lord, in the passage from Matthew, both gives precedence to the love of God—"the first and greatest commandment"—and establishes an essential link between love of God and love of neighbor. You can't have one without the other.

We cannot love our neighbor without first knowing the love of God, and we cannot say we love God without manifesting that love in love for our neighbor.

And this is his commandment, that we should believe in the name of his Son Jesus Christ and love one another, just as he has commanded us. All who keep his commandments abide in him and he in them. And by this we know that he abides in us, by the Spirit which he has given us.

(I John 3:23-24)

Beloved, let us love one another; for love is of God, and he who loves is born of God and knows God. He who does not love does not know God; for God is love. In this the love of God was made manifest among us, that God sent his only Son into the world, so that we might live through him. In this is love, not that we loved God but that he loved us and sent his Son to be the expiation of our sins. Beloved, if God so loved us, we also ought to love one another. No man has ever seen God; if we love one another, God abides in us and his love is perfected in us. By this we know that we abide in him and he in us, because he has given us of his own Spirit.

(I John 4:7-13)

In reality, the two loves, as John's letters underscore, are really one. It's not that we love God and manage to be nice to our neighbor as a pious extra. Nor is the idea here that it's really about caring for other people—that's the essential thing—and if loving God helps you to do that, fine. Loving God first, as the source and origin of our love for others, means that we will love our neighbor on the basis of His unconditional love and commitment to them and in the power of His Spirit. Our love for neighbor, without the empowerment of God's love, will be essentially inadequate, even under the best of circumstances—tainted by self-interest and human inconstancy.

In fact, the whole process of the spiritual life is meant to form in us, day by day, the character of Jesus, so that our response to our world is His response to it, our presence in the lives of our family and friends marked with the character of His presence and mercy.

This is why the first step in building Christian brotherhood in any context—parish, community, convent, support group—is, and must be, personal surrender to the Lord. It all starts with opening up to the love of God and the power of His Spirit.

Not that loving God is a means to an end. Loving God is the one essential end, the very purpose of human existence: "Man is created to praise, reverence, and serve God our Lord." (St. Ignatius of Loyola, *Spiritual Exercises,* First Principle and Foundation) "You have made us for yourself, Lord, and our hearts are restless until they rest in you." (St. Augustine, *Confessions*)

Covenant Love

The kind of love God has for us, and which we are called to mirror in our love for others, is *covenant love.* The word the Hebrew Scriptures use to describe this essential characteristic of God's love is "*hesed,*" a word that is frequently (and incompletely) translated as "mercy" or "loving kindness" in English translations of the Bible.

The importance of characterizing God with this word can be gauged by the fact that it appears 245 times in the Old Testament and more than 127 times in the Psalms alone.

The Revised Standard Version (RSV) is closer to the mark when it translates *hesed* as "steadfast love" or "loyalty." *Hesed* indicates God's merciful fidelity to His covenant promises, despite the fickleness of His human partners. (Covenant, or *berith* in Hebrew, stands for "chain" or "binding pledge".) God's loyalty to His covenant, even in the face of human sin and betrayal, means life for His people; it also grounds the gift of His mercy, not in concession or indulgence, but in the very nature of His being—in His name, which is Love:

And the Lord descended in the cloud and stood with [Moses] there, and proclaimed the name of the Lord. The Lord passed by him and proclaimed, "the Lord, the Lord, a God merciful and gracious, slow to anger, and abounding in steadfast love and faithfulness (hesed)." (Exodus 34:5-6)

This teaching receives one of its most compelling expressions in Psalm 103:

My soul, give thanks to the Lord and never forget all his blessings:

It is he who forgives all your guilt, who heals every one of your ills,

who redeems your life from the grave,

who crowns you with love

and compassion,

who fills your life with good things,

renewing your youth like an eagle's.

The Lord is compassion and love, slow to anger and rich in mercy.

His wrath will come to an end; He will not be angry forever.

He does not treat us according to our sins

nor repay us according to our faults.

For as the heavens are high above the earth

so strong is his love for those who fear him.

As far as the east is from the west

so far does he remove our sins.

(Psalm 103:2-5, 8-12)

God's covenant love, of course, finds its ultimate expression—its incarnation—in the words and deeds of His Son, Jesus Christ, who loved and redeemed mankind even in the face of His death on the cross and who raised the human race to new life in Him at His resurrection.

God shows his love for us in that while we were yet sinners Christ died for us....For if while we were enemies we were reconciled to God by the death of his Son, much more, now that we are reconciled, shall we be saved by his life. (Romans 5:8, 10)

If God is for us, who can be against us? He who did not spare his own Son, but gave him up for us all, will he not also give us all things with him?...Who shall separate us from the love of Christ? Shall tribulation, or distress, or persecution, or famine, nakedness, peril, or sword?...No, in all these things, we are more than conquerors through him who loved us. For I am sure that neither death nor life nor angels nor principalities, nor things present, nor things to come, nor powers, nor height, nor depth, nor anything else in all creation, will be able to separate us from the love of God in Christ Jesus our Lord. (Romans 8:31-39)

The call to love God and neighbor as the Gospels envision is not something achieved overnight, or through a single experience, however inspired; it is the work of a lifetime; its challenges remain daunting until we draw our last breath, dependent from beginning to end on God's abundant grace and on the help of those God has placed in our lives.

Some common cultural attitudes can complicate our response to the call of covenant love.

Contract vs. Covenant

In the past, many important relationships in people's lives—marriage, family life, national ties, church affiliation—bore a covenantal stamp. This reflected, in some cases, the residual effects of Judeo-Christian thought in general society. By covenant, I mean a personal relationship characterized by commitment and fidelity to another person or institution, even if (or when) loving the other or being faithful to that relationship entails personal suffering and loss. In its essence, covenant is radically other-focused on the health, welfare, and salvation of others. Covenant, as its Hebrew root implies (*berith* or chain), has the negative sense of binding us, preventing us from doing whatever we will, and the positive sense of holding us and our deepest investments in place even in the midst of the vicissitudes of life. This, as we have considered, is the way God loves, the character of His *hesed*, or steadfast love.

Contractual thinking, on the other hand, is characterized by provisional commitments: I agree to love this person or be loyal to this institution in accordance with certain expectations, determined on the basis of whether he or she, or it responds to my perceived needs. In other words: Is this good (or still good) for me? Is it meeting (or still meeting) my needs? If circumstances or expectations change, or should unanticipated difficulties arise, this may require renegotiating the terms of the relationship, or result in its dissolution and a renewed search for a more suitable (or fulfilling) object of affection.

Clearly, the contractual model, with its focus on self-determined personal fulfillment, on hedging one's bets, and negotiable terms, has largely displaced the echoes of covenantal understanding in much of today's culture—and with unmistakable effects. The modern elastic marriage seems an increasingly brittle affair. (Little wonder, then, that as time goes by even the provisional charms of the contractual marriage seem daunting for many young couples today). Family breakdown and the resulting erosion of covenantal commitment to children and elderly persons is fast becoming a serious social evil. Even loyalty to the Church today, to serious religious commitments, often seems focused on whether needs are being met rather than on whether people are being called to contribute and serve.

Perhaps the contrast between contractual and covenant love is best illustrated by a few examples:

A young couple, wed just after World War II, faced a severe crisis early on in their marriage. The husband contracted polio and was subsequently paralyzed from the waist down. They had just begun their life together, and the wife was pregnant with their first and only child. Clearly, this devastating turn of events was not part of their plans, or something they could have anticipated, and it meant accepting a very different sort of marriage than the one they had been looking forward to. For the husband, it meant disability and limitation for the rest of his life, and for his wife, a challenging lifelong role as a caregiver. But because they were people of faith, with a covenantal understanding of marriage—for better or for worse, in sickness or in health—they made the difficult and loving adjustment to new circumstances and lived to find in those circumstances life, purpose, and mission—along with the grace of the compassionate Christ.

A young woman from a close Catholic family took care of her younger brother, who had severe mental disabilities. When his care became impossible to manage at home, the family placed the brother in a Catholic care facility, but his sister continued to spend much of each day with him, ensuring that his ties to home and family remained constant. Eventually, she decided not to marry in order to carry out this daunting service to her brother. In return for her commitment, the family provided for her financial needs. Over time, she became the angel of the care facility, as generous in her concern for other patients as she was for her brother—the person who always remembered birthdays and Christmas, the one who paid special attention to those who had no family, and a comfort and support to the staff.

All covenantal relationships share this same dynamic: through the grace of covenant fidelity, they weather the death of dreams and the failure of expectations. Constancy brings deeper levels of commitment, understanding, and spiritual maturity and, ultimately, a share in God's own fidelity, kindness, and mercy.

They also, it should be noted, have capacities for embracing the poor, the sick, and for an inclusive embrace of people who are not like us—always to our enrichment as persons—that fly in the face of the narrow self-focused confines of the contractual model.

In the context of building brotherhood and sisterhood, it is vital to re-

alize and acknowledge that our relationships with fellow Catholics—whether in parish, or convent, or community—are covenantal relationships.** Through baptism, we are brothers and sisters in Christ, and the quality of our relationships needs to reflect this fact: that we are covenantally bound to one another. This familial reality is, of course, already reflected in the language we use: We call priests "father"; we are addressed during the Mass as "brothers and sisters"; we hear Scripture readings that highlight the familial character of Christian relationships. But this covenantal reality must become a great deal more than mere language. Its demands must shape the character of the way we actually relate to each other—and this, beyond considerations of temperament, class, or interests. Too often, relationships in parishes or in other Catholic contexts have a more functional character than covenantal one—we do various activities together. A great part of building brotherhood and sisterhood in any social context has to do with making the shift from functional to covenantal relationships.

The Myth of Emotional Authenticity

Another cultural problem that can affect our approach to loving our brothers and sisters has to do with the notion of love as feeling.

Popular culture has inevitably had (and continues to have) a great influence on common notions about the nature of love. Love is often characterized in our society as a feeling, as a certain kind of positive emotional response rather than as a way of living and acting.

This plays an outsized role in modern notions of love in marriage. How many movies has one seen in which the husband wakes up one morning to realize that he no longer has feelings for his wife—that he no longer feels the same way he did about her when he first married her? He concludes, naturally, that to remain in the marriage under these circumstances would be dishonest and hypocritical, and, promptly sets about arranging its (hopefully) amicable end.

While emotions are a profound part of what makes us human, positive emotions are not the central reality of love in a Christian sense—they are not the motivating agent. A Christian hardly needs to wait for an overpowering emotion in order to serve the elderly neighbor down the block, or, conversely, to feel that his or her service to the food pantry is wanting or inauthentic because it doesn't evoke powerful feelings; or, as in our previous example, that the absence of passion necessarily means that a marriage is dead. As we have seen, **Chris-**

tian love is decisively embodied in committed personal relationships, empowered by the Holy Spirit, and expressed in care, concern, dedication and service. It's primarily a matter of action, not emotion.

Love Your Neighbor

The writer CS Lewis once observed: "I do not even always enjoy my own society. So apparently 'love your neighbor' does not mean 'feel fond of him' or 'find him attractive.'"

This does not mean that Christian love, though rooted in the will, is merely dutiful or impersonal. On the contrary, it should be expressed with affection, warmth, and sensitivity to the person and situation involved. Scripture itself clothes the word mercy (or covenant love) with implications of tenderness. The point is that while emotions support and enrich our moral decisions, they don't decide or determine them.

One of the biggest problems we tend to have in this area is the distaste our culture has bred into us about duty and obligation. "I don't want you to bother coming to see me," an elderly woman once told her daughter, "if it's just a duty."

Of course, there may have been a way in which the daughter communicated that visiting her mother was a burden or an unpleasant task. But our culture for some decades has highlighted so-called "emotional authenticity", the idea that one should only do those things one feels deeply about at the moment, or which constitute matters of strictly personal choice, outside the realm of obligation or ethical demand.

Older cultures would have found (and do find) this notion quite curious. In more traditional cultures, the elderly count on their children's sense of filial duty to ease the insecurities of old age; children count on the commitment of adults to shield them from harm; spouses count on a mutual sense of loyalty to protect their marriage from the ravages of infidelity.

Building brotherhood and sisterhood in Christ means recovering the importance of *duty*—it's really not a bad word—and unlearning some of the conceptual prejudices we have inherited from the culture, particularly about the primacy of emotions in determining relationships and what we do in them.

Again, this brings us back to the covenant idea. One always hopes that there's more to relationships than mere obligation. But even a sense of obligation to one's spouse or children contains within it devotion as well as duty, concern as well as covenant. A sense of covenantal loyalty is there to keep us grounded in what is most important to us, in the fundamental investments we have made in life amid the many changes in circumstance, attitude, and outlook that occur in a lifetime.

One of the most exemplary acts of love recorded in Scripture is instructive, reflecting many of the themes we've been considering: the Parable of the Good Samaritan.

Jesus tells the famous parable in the context of His teaching on the love of God and neighbor we quoted at the beginning of this chapter. (Luke 10:25-28) The lawyer who had asked the initial question, "What shall I do to inherit eternal life?" had, on being directed by Christ to give the right answer to his own question, followed up with another: "And who is my neighbor?"

Jesus tells the parable in reply.

You know the story. A Jew going from Jerusalem to Jericho falls victim to robbers on the road who leave him for dead. A priest and a Levite pass by, but, likely due to ritual purity laws, fail to come to his aid. Only a Samaritan, whom Jews would consider a foreigner and a religious schismatic, has compassion on him and sees to the man's care. (Luke 10:30-32)

The Samaritan goes to the victim, binds his wounds, places him on his own beast of burden, brings him to an inn, and nurses him there. The next day, the Samaritan pays the innkeeper to provide for the man in his absence. (Luke 10:33-35)

Two things are significant for our purposes in this parable:

1. The Lord indicates that the neighbor, the object of the commandment to love, transcends typical human boundaries to embrace even perceived enemies and opponents. If that's the case, the commandment to love surely includes all sorts of people who are not my preferred company, who don't belong to my circle and with whom I have little in common, who don't share my views on religious or social questions, who don't meet my expectations, and, even more challenging, who might not even appreciate (or be able to appreciate) my attempts to love them.

2. And most importantly, the Lord's description of the Samaritan's compassion is focused on caring actions. We are told that he bound up wounds, administered healing, and provided for his long-term care. In other words, he

24

loved him.

When Jesus had told his parable, he asked the lawyer whose question had inspired it, to provide the moral, the point of the story.

"Which of these three [the priest, the Levite, or the Samaritan], do you think, proved neighbor to the man who fell among the robbers?" He said, "The one who showed mercy on him." *And Jesus said, "Go and* do *likewise."* (Luke 10:36-37)*

Interestingly, the Greek word for *mercy* used here is *eleos*, the New Testament equivalent for the Hebrew word *hesed* (steadfast love). And note that Jesus does not urge his listeners to cultivate tender feelings toward others, but to manifest mercy in deeds.

The Parable of the Good Samaritan is not only a moving story of compassion. It is a portrait of covenant love.

Things to Think and Pray About

The shift from contractual or provisional notions of relationship to that of covenant is the key to living the way of Christian love.

➡ Our relationships with fellow Catholics are not functional but covenantal relationships.

➡ Covenant love is founded on actions, not feelings.

➡ Building brotherhood and sisterhood in Christ means recovering the importance of duty.

➡ The first and most fundamental obstacle to love is inconvenience.

➡ The only way love for God and others can grow is from self-knowledge. This, most often, is the fruit of our failures. Knowing the extent of our self-love fosters humility. Knowing of God's unconditional and steadfast love for us fosters love for God and for others.

Endnote [1]: **Shema Yisrael** (or **Sh'ma Yisrael**; "Hear, O Israel") are the first two words of a section of the Torah, and is the title (sometimes shortened to simply **Shema**) of a prayer that serves as a centerpiece of the morning and evening Jewish prayer services. The first word encapsulates the monotheistic essence of Judaism: "Hear O Israel, the LORD our God, the LORD is one," found in Deuteronomy 6:4, sometimes alternately translated as "The LORD our God, the LORD alone."

Chapter 2
Building a Spiritual Culture

*Just as we are obliged to approach matters of doctrinal truth
with a thoroughly and distinctively Christian mind, guided by
revelation...so we are obliged to live a thoroughly and distinctively Christian way of life, incarnating Christian truth in the concrete details of our daily tasks and relationships.*

Mark Kinzer, from "Christian Identity and Social
Change in Technological Society," in *Christianity Confronts
Modernity*, Servant Books, 1981

C hristianity is a way of being in the world. While contemporary Christians frequently occupy themselves with developing new approach-
es to spirituality and enriching liturgy, with exploring the ramifications of the new technology for evangelization—all eminently worthy concerns—too little thought is given to the single most pressing concern any
Christian has: **living the Gospel as a way of life.**

Love: The Heart of a Spiritual Culture

When I attended meetings in the 1980s on the cultural challenges facing
Christianity, I heard about models of engagement with the broader secular culture, or with efforts to defend Christian truth against the Gospel's modern rivals.
But few people seemed to grasp the greater challenge of rebuilding the internal
life of Catholics—how to live our daily lives in the light and power of the Gospel,
how to live in practical terms as brothers and sisters in Christ, according to what
might well be called the internal "spiritual culture" of Christianity itself.

All outward-focused aspects of the Church (evangelization, social mission,
the apostolate) flow from this: vital Christian families and neighborhoods. And
this seemed the one topic most people, mistakenly, took for granted.

A classic example: much of the focus on inspiring new vocations to the
priesthood and the religious life seems fixed on lively advertising or seminary
reform—necessary and useful—but it neglects the need to renew and restore
the Catholic family out of which such vocations come. If the Catholic family is
not a living reality—a domestic church, as St. John Chrysostom calls it, a place
of worship and evangelization—the other efforts can hardly be expected to
make up for such a fundamental deficiency.

It is imperative that we take sober stock of where we really are, historically,

26

and what is really happening around us. By the latter part of the 20th century, intact Christian neighborhoods, once the backbone of parishes, were a rarity. Job requirements, educational and economic opportunity, the individualistic nature of the American dream, all contributed to creating a highly mobile society with few real and lasting commitments. Eventually, family life itself failed to cohere. It became ships passing in the night, a loose assemblage of largely functional relationships.

These social changes affected parish life as well, reducing it from a gathering of people living daily Christian life together in their neighborhoods and communities into a largely functional environment in which parishioners, typically, have minimal relational contact and little practical support meeting the real challenges of Christian life. What should be done when people lose their jobs, when families face bereavement, when young parents need help, when children are in crisis.

More than anything else, it was this insight, this recognition that fueled the emergence of lay communities in the charismatic renewal: that all the Holy Spirit was giving and teaching us in the renewal was leading and equipping us to be brothers and sisters in the real world, equipping us to love and serve in the midst of all the challenges of the modern age. *Love is the destination of the charisms, the purpose for which they have been given.* This is the theme of one of the most famous Scripture passages:

> If I speak in the tongues of men and angels, but have not love, I am a noisy gong or a clanging cymbal. And if I have prophetic powers and understand all mysteries and all knowledge, and if I have all faith, so as to remove mountains, but have not love, I am nothing. If I give away all I have, and if I deliver my body to be burned, but have not love, I gain nothing.

So we get the idea that love in the Pauline sense is not some kind of vague sentiment, but real behavior in real time:

> Love is patient and kind; love is not jealous or boastful; it is not arrogant or rude. Love does not insist on its own way; it is not irritable or resentful; it does not rejoice at wrong, but rejoices in the right. Love bears all things, hopes all things, endures all things. Love never ends. (I Corinthians 13:1-8)

This love that Paul speaks of is the heart of the spiritual culture, the internal, defining culture of Catholic life.

What Is a Spiritual Culture?

First of all, culture is a design for living, a way of life that encompasses the whole breadth and range of the human enterprise—morality, personal relations, family, courtship, celebration and mourning, sanctity of time, conflict resolution, piety, manners. Culture is not about a limited set of activities in the modern sense of leisure pursuits or entertainment, but the whole of life. Hence, Greek culture designates the Greek way of life, how Greeks approach the whole range of human interests and activities.

What I am suggesting is that Catholics have a culture in this sense, too. Not an ethnic culture, but a universal spiritual culture, one pertaining to every Catholic, that includes the moral dimension, how Catholics should behave. It goes on to embrace the practical implications, in real life circumstances, of being a baptized person and living the life to which the sacraments point, and which they empower. This quotation aptly captures this sense of integration of sacramental life with real behavior:

> It is evident that all our spiritual strength ought to be employed against ourselves, against our own inclinations, against our natural aversions, against our cowardice, against the horror of all that crosses us... against all in us that resists God....*If we acquire more mastery over ourselves, if we are less touchy and sensitive, more generous in undertaking, more patient in suffering, more faithful to our good resolutions, more indifferent to the esteem or contempt of men, more obedient to all the impulses of divine grace, more ready for all the sacrifices God asks of us, this is an infallible proof of the goodness of our Communions.* (Rev. Jean-Nicholas Grou, SJ, 1803)*

Or this more modern celebration of the union of sacramental grace and the details of ordinary life:

> Our life is sacramental. We do not live that peculiar thing one hears so much of, a "spiritual life." We live a natural and supernatural life; we live it through the medium of the simplest substance of things. Our Lord gave Himself to us through our flesh and blood; we give ourselves back to Him through it. The symbols of the gift of His own life are bread, wine, water and oil. *We give our life back to Him through the dust He made us out of, through everything we see and touch and taste and hear, the food we eat, the clothes we wear, the words we speak, the sleep we sleep. Such are the sacramentals of our love, things ordinary with the ordinariness of the*

risen Christ. (Caryll Houselander, 1950)*

Such a universal culture, formed by the sacraments, is a spiritual culture, that is, one inspired, shaped, graced and sustained by the Holy Spirit.

All too often, people today tend of think of the word *spiritual* as either

1. immaterial—something opposed to the physical, as in a spiritual connection with a person, or, worse,

2. descriptive of a vague set of personal beliefs set in opposition to commitment to a religious tradition ("I am *spiritual*, not religious").

Spiritual in the New Testament sense has to do with the work of the Holy Spirit, whose purpose is to form in us the character of Christ and teach us the culture of the kingdom.

Basic to the character of that spiritual culture, of that receptivity to the work of the Holy Spirit, is a commitment to change. Undergirding all that this book attempts to outline is the call to a *repentant life*—a life formed by the desire to change, to turn away from a life shaped by the darkness of this age to one formed in the image of Christ and His kingdom.

> *I appeal to you, therefore, brethren, by the mercies of God, to present your bodies [selves] as a living sacrifice, holy and acceptable to God, which is your spiritual worship.* Do not be conformed to this world [age] but be transformed by the renewal of your mind, that you may prove what is the will of God, what is good and acceptable and perfect. (Romans 12:1-2)*

> Put off your old nature which belongs to your former manner of life and is corrupt through deceitful lusts, and be renewed in the spirit of your minds, and put on the new nature, created after the likeness of God in true righteousness and holiness. (Ephesians 4:22-24)*

Repentance is not a one-time thing, or something we do only when we've fallen into serious sin, or during Lent, but a commitment to change that marks the character of our whole Christian life. The original Hebrew word for *repentance*, used in the Old Testament, and reflected dramatically in the language of the Parable of the Prodigal Son (Luke 15:17-18), is *teshuvah*, a word meaning "to turn." Our whole Christian life is a process of turning *away* from the darkness of sin and death and *toward* the light of Christ in every aspect of our lives.

I heard a speaker make this analogy some years ago that makes this notion of a culture of repentance more concrete:

It is as if (according to the analogy) we are all kidnap victims, children abducted from our true home and held captive by an evil master. In this environment, under the reign of our abductor, every sort of abuse occurs: we are kept in confined spaces, starved, beaten, and live in constant terror.

Our brother, who has been desperately searching for us, eventually locates the den of the abductor, decisively defeats the villain, rescues us from our terrible captivity, and brings us home to be with him.

We are now free, no longer subject to the evil whims of our captor. We are living in the new kingdom, our destined home, with our brother (Christ). But the years of captivity have taken their toll. Our experiences in the darkness still shape and haunt us. Our characters have been twisted by the years of abuse and cruelty. Despite the safety and security of our new environment, we still find ourselves rebelling against the constraints of love and care, preferring instead the dark patterns taught to us in our captivity.

And the abductor himself, though defeated, still lurks in the darkness, attempting to lure us back to his domain, sending us messages to mistrust our rescuer and his motives, encouraging us to believe the thoughts and perceptions with which he has so long deceived us.

It is our brother's task, the Lord's task, and the work of His Spirit, to teach us, moment by moment, day by day, a new way of life, recalling us to our family origins and our true nature. He is teaching us step by step how to behave, how to live in the home in which we truly belong. He is weaning us, bit by bit, from the patterns we learned in the darkness and all its insidious effects, training us with patience and compassion in the life of the kingdom.

Things to Think and Pray About

The challenge of changing relational patterns—the lifework of repentance—can only be realized in submission to the loving power of the Holy Spirit and requires the support of Christian brothers and sisters who are also committed to being "inspired, shaped, graced and sustained by the Holy Spirit."

- "We are obliged to live a thoroughly and distinctively Christian way of life, incarnating Christian truth in the concrete details of our daily tasks and relationships." (Mark Kinzer)

- Catholics have a universal spiritual culture, one that embraces the practical implications of being a baptized person.

- Receptivity to the work of the Holy Spirit means a commitment to change.

- "We give our life back to Him...through everything we see and touch and taste and hear....Such are the sacramentals of our love, things ordinary with the ordinariness of the risen Christ." (Caryll Houselander)

- "Commitment in a community is not primarily something active, like joining a political party or trade union. [Community] is the recognition by its members that they have been called by God to live together, love each other, pray and work together in response to the cry of the poor. And that comes first at the level of being rather than of doing." (Jean Vanier, *Community and Growth*)

Part 2
The Building Blocks of Spiritual Culture

Introduction: Part 2—The Building Blocks of Spiritual Culture

Let's start with a disclaimer. In these next six chapters we'll study the building blocks of spiritual culture. I'm not proposing to give a full treatment of these essential topics. Instead, I've laid out core principles with the hope that these biblical and traditional perspectives will stir readers to examine their own relationships in the context of their particular circumstances. I'll let the chips fall where they may, letting these hard and life-giving truths speak for themselves. If we approach them with open and honest hearts, asking for the Lord's help and guidance and the support of our families and fellow Christians with whom we live, He will show us how to incorporate these truths, bit by bit, day by day, situation by situation, into our lives. This is a life-long process, full of false starts and mistakes. But it's no less of a work of the Holy Spirit, forming in us the character of Christ and teaching us the holy and redeeming art of everyday love.

Chapter 3

Right Speech

Death and life are in the power of the tongue.

Proverbs 18:21

It may come as something of a surprise that right speech shows up at the top of the list of the building blocks of a spiritual culture. A little reflection on our own experiences will show that no moral aspiration can long endure or be much more, in practical terms, than sentiment unless the way we speak to each other is converted. It must be transformed from the toxic and destructive patterns of the world into life-giving speech of the kingdom of God.

A Matter of Life and Death

Considering the biblical vision of the way God's people should and should not speak, I remember being dismayed by the way we "religious" people spoke to and about one another. We might be full of idealism and good intentions; we might worship together with great fervor; but we also routinely used bad language, belittled one another, and gossiped at every available opportunity—with predictable results: We did not and could not trust each other. This strange "schizophrenia" —the earnest quest for unity and brotherhood coupled with relational habits that rendered this impossible—affects many of our environments: family, church, convent, parish council, and ministry.

The centrality of speech to the whole Christian enterprise was brought home to me many years ago in the context of a talk on right speech I gave to a diverse group of renewal leaders. At the end of the talk, an older religious sister came up to me and said simply and with great sadness, "I can't tell you the tragedies my convent would have been spared had we heard and applied this teaching."

In my experience, if speech patterns do not begin to be confronted and redeemed, then nothing else that we do or attempt as Christians will be effective in the long run. If we're to start anywhere to build a spiritual culture, we have to start here.

The way we speak to one another and about one another is a matter of life and death. (Proverbs 18:21) We have the power to "create" or destroy others with our tongues, with the way we employ the gift of speech.

The first task is to get it into our heads how serious this area really is, and how deficient most of us are when our speech habits are compared with the biblical and traditional ideal. The nearly universal tendency where we hear scriptural passages about speech is to deflect (and thus resist) the impact with "yes, buts," and excuses of various sorts. If we're to gain anything from these reflections, we must begin by ceasing to defend ourselves and instead listen with an open heart to God's Word.

Curse the whisperer and deceiver, for he has destroyed many who were at peace. Slander has shaken many and scattered them from nation to nation, and destroyed strong cities and overturned the houses of great men. Slander has driven away courageous women, and deprived them of the fruit of their toil. Whoever pays heed to slander will not find rest, nor will he settle down in peace. The blow of a whip raises a welt, but a blow of the tongue crushes the bones. Many have fallen by the edge of the sword, but not so many as have fallen because of the tongue....*See that you fence in your property with thorns, lock up your silver and gold, make balances and scales for your words and make a door and a bolt for your mouth. Beware lest you err with your tongue, lest you fall before him who lies in wait.* (Sirach 28:13-18, 24-26)*

This Old Testament realism about the power and far-reaching effects of speech is echoed in the New Testament as well.

So the tongue is a little member and boasts of great things. How great a forest is set ablaze by a small fire! And the tongue is a fire. The tongue is an unrighteous world among our members, staining the whole body, setting on fire the cycle of nature and set on fire by hell. For every kind of beast and bird, of reptile and sea creature can be tamed and has been tamed by humankind, but no human being can tame the tongue—a restless evil, full of deadly poison. With it we bless the Lord and Father, and with it we curse men, who are made in the image and likeness of God. From the same mouth come blessing and cursing. My brethren, this ought not to be so. Does a spring pour forth from the same opening fresh water and brackish? (James 3:5-11)

To Love God and Be in His Presence

Learning appropriate speech habits is part of what it means to love God and be in His presence, as is reflected in this psalm:

Lord, who shall be admitted to your tent

And dwell on your holy mountain?

He who walks without fault;

he who acts with justice

and speaks the truth from his heart;

he who does not slander with his tongue;

he who does no wrong to his brother,

who casts no slur upon his neighbor,

who holds the godless in disdain,

but honors those who fear the Lord;

he who keeps his pledge, come what may;

who takes no interest on a loan

and accepts no bribes against the innocent.

Such a man will stand firm forever. (Psalm 15)*

This psalm describes a procession entering the Temple, and asks on what basis people are admitted into God's presence. In verse two, the psalmist replies, laying out a list of behaviors that qualify (and disqualify) a person from being in the presence of the Lord. Interestingly, few of the requirements listed by the Psalmist have to do with what we would call "spirituality". There's not much mysticism here. The psalmist pointedly stresses what we might well call practical ethics: justice, reliability, ethical conduct in finances, and, in particular, speech. He emphasizes speaking the truth, avoiding slander and detraction. Simply put, the psalmist is saying that we can't love and worship the just God while routinely committing injustice against our brothers and sisters; that we can't function as His people without godly speech; that it matters to God if we're committing injustice against our neighbor with our tongue. It's analogous to Christ's admonition in the Sermon on the Mount, that forgiveness and reconciliation constitute a precondition for worship.

"If you are offering your gift at the altar, and there remember that your brother has something against you, leave your gift there before the altar and go; first be reconciled with your brother, and then come and offer your gift." (Matthew 5:23-25)

In the same way, we have to strive to adopt God's standards in the area of speech, to learn His justice in this area, or we're in no position to worship Him effectively or model His image to the world.

Our Speech Is Meant to Be a Source of Life

The mouth of the righteous is a fountain of life, *but the mouth of the wicked conceals violence....When words are many, transgression is not lacking, but he who restrains his lips is prudent....The tongue of the righteous is choice silver....The* lips of the righteous feed many, *but fools die for lack of sense....The* mouth of the righteous brings forth wisdom.... *The lips of the righteous know what is acceptable, but the mouth of the wicked, what is perverse.... There is one whose rash words are like sword thrusts, but* the tongue of the wise brings healing. (Proverbs 10:11, 19-21, 31, 32; 12:18)*

The speech culture with which God wishes to equip us is a speech that imparts life, wisdom, nourishment, enrichment and healing to others—speech, in other words, that serves as an instrument of God's love, truth, mercy and salvation in people's lives.

In the Hebrew Prophets, God promised that when the Messiah came, among the changes he would bring would be a change in way people speak to each other.

At that time, I will change the speech of the peoples to a pure speech, *that all of them may call upon the name of the Lord and serve him with one accord....On that day, you shall not be put to shame because of the deeds by which you have rebelled against me; for then I will remove from your midst your proudly exultant ones, and you shall no longer be haughty on my holy mountain. For I will leave in the midst of you a people humble and lowly....They shall do no wrong and utter no lies, nor shall there be found in their mouth a deceitful tongue.* (Zephaniah 3:9-13)*

Blasphemy, lying, and arrogant or boastful speech are not part of the culture of God's kingdom. Instead, the speech of the kingdom is characterized by humility, which is a commonly misunderstood word today. Humility, in the biblical sense, is not a matter of low self-esteem and cast-down eyes, but of service. *The speech of the kingdom is a speech that seeks to serve.*

Unity in the Body of Christ Is Built on the Foundation of Godly Speech

I therefore, a prisoner for the Lord, beg you to lead a life worthy of the call-ing to which you have been called, with all lowliness and meekness, with patience, forbearing one another in love, eager to maintain the unity of the Spirit in the bond of peace...*Put off your old nature which belongs to your former manner of life and is corrupt through deceitful lusts, and be renewed in the spirit of your minds, and put on* the new nature, created after the like-ness of God *in true righteousness and holiness. Therefore, putting away falsehood, let everyone speak the truth with his neighbor, for we are mem-bers one of another...Let no evil talk come out of your mouths, but only such as is good for edifying, as fits the occasion, that it may impart grace to those who hear...Let all bitterness and wrath and anger and clamor and slander be put away from you, with all malice, and be kind to one another, tenderheart-ed, forgiving one another, as God in Christ forgave you.* (Ephesians 4:1-3, 22-25, 29, 31, 32)

The theme of this chapter in Paul's Letter to the Ephesians is unity, the uni-ty that the Spirit produces in the Church. Notice that Paul urges us to be eager to *maintain* (that is, "preserve" or "guard") that unity. In other words, unity in the Church, including its parish, small group, or other local manifestation, is some-thing that needs to be guarded. The Spirit indeed brings unity, but we, too, play a role. There are things we need to do to foster the unity of the Spirit, and things we need to avoid. Paul goes on in the letter to describe behaviors that contrib-ute to the preservation of unity, and behaviors that harm it.

Speech plays a large role in fostering unity and a large role in dismantling it: (to paraphrase) let no evil talk come out of your mouths, but only such talk as builds up (or edifies) the body of Christ. How we speak to and about one anoth-er can reinforce or strengthen the unity that God is building among us or weak-en it, even tear it apart.

If the importance of speech needs further amplification, then, let Jesus Himself have the last word:

"I tell you, on the Day of Judgment, men will render account for every care-less word they utter; for by your words you will be justified, and by your words you will be condemned." (Matthew 12:36-37)

Common Problems of Speech

Sobered by that alarming prospect, let's talk about some common problems of speech. We'll start with the most obvious ones:

Lying

Lying is making an untrue statement with the intent to deceive or to create a false and misleading impression. Most people recognize outright deception as a serious wrong. It's a sin against the Eighth Commandment (bearing false witness against your neighbor). But there are more subtle varieties of deception or duplicity. One can use an innocent remark to create a misleading impression about someone or to enhance your own reputation at the expense of another. One can imply that his contribution was the deciding factor in a positive outcome when he, in fact, knows differently. Or, we can mask our own views in remarks attributed to others (*i.e.,* "My friends tell me that..."). Scripture calls us to be a people of straightforward, honest, and loyal speech. (Proverbs 12:17-22; Matthew 5:33-37; Ephesians 4:25)

Murmuring, Grumbling, and Complaining

This problem shouldn't require much explanation. We all do it. But besides noting the toxic environment a steady diet of negative speech creates, Scripture urges us to look at the serious spiritual problems underlying habitual murmuring and complaining. Upon their liberation from bondage in Egypt, the people of Israel **murmured** in the desert against Moses and even against God Himself, not only as they encountered various hardships in the journey to the Promised Land, but also because God's provisions did not always meet their expectations. (Numbers 11:1) The Old Testament does not hesitate to call this murmuring "unbelief." (Numbers 14:11) (See I Corinthians 10:9-10, as well.)

It is, as biblical scholar Xavier Leon Dufour has written, a type of fear, which demands from God an immediate realization of His promises; that wants to reduce God to an assuager of personal anxieties, whose main function in the universe is to provide for my perceived needs and desires. It's no accident that Israel's murmurers were the principal agents in the creation of the Golden Calf. Hence, one becomes angered when realization is delayed, or when wants appear to be unmet.

To resist the culture of complaint, as Paul observes in Philippians, is an act of faith in God and His Word:

Do all things without grumbling or questioning, that you may be blameless and innocent, children of God without blemish in the midst of a crooked and perverse generation, among whom you shine as lights in the world, holding fast the word of life. (Philippians 2:14-16a)

Gossiping

When we think about gossip, it's easy to evade the seriousness of it with excuses, like:

– Well, it's wrong to do it, of course, but it's just idle talk.

The Book of Leviticus takes a tougher line on the subject. It satirizes the gossiper as a peddler of tales, displaying his merchandise in the market; and, not incidentally, it equates such trafficking in confidences with murder:

You shall not go up and down as a slanderer [Hebrew *rochil* means "talebearer"] *among your people, and you shall not stand forth against the blood [or life] of your neighbor.* (Leviticus 19:16)

The letter to the Romans makes the same sobering comparison. Paul is describing the consequences in pagan society of the refusal to acknowledge the truth about God:

They were filled with all manner of wickedness, evil, covetousness, malice. Full of envy, murder, strife, deceit, malignity, they are gossips, slanderers, haters of God, insolent, haughty, boastful, inventors of evil, disobedient to parents, foolish, faithless, heartless, ruthless. (Romans 1:29-31)

Like Leviticus, Paul puts gossip in a list with murder. Gossip—the spreading of rumors of an intimate nature about somebody—can, in fact, *murder* a person's reputation, character, and commitment.

Detraction is a kind of murder....The detractor, by a single stroke of his tongue, ordinarily commits three murders: He kills his own soul and that of him who listens to him by a spiritual murder, and he takes away the social life of him who he defames. (Saint Francis de Sales, *Introduction to the Devout Life*)

Gossiping betrays confidences and damages relationships:

He who goes about gossiping reveals secrets; therefore, do not associate with one who speaks foolishly. (Proverbs 20:19)

For a wound may be bandaged, and there is reconciliation after abuse, but whoever has betrayed secrets is without hope.
(Sirach 20:27:21)

A perverse man spreads strife, and a whisperer separates close friends.
(Proverbs 16:28)

He who goes about as a talebearer reveals secrets, but he who is trustworthy keeps a thing hidden. (Proverbs 11:13)*

While many of us try to avoid outright gossiping, it's easy to justify aspects of gossiping under the rubric of "curiosity"—otherwise known as being a "busybody," someone who goes around attending to other people's affairs and who becomes a source for inside information on people.

- "Now I know you might not feel free to talk about this openly, but I was just wondering whether you know why Sally is so unhappy?"
- "I'm curious, did the police investigation of the deacon's son ever go anywhere?"

Being a busybody involves curiosity and speculation about others' lives for whom we have no direct responsibility. Thus, it is a form of gossip. A simple approach to the lure of curiosity: *if you're not part of the problem, or part of the solution, stay out of other people's business.*

Confidentiality is a related issue. Most people understand that it's a serious thing to reveal to others what has been told you in confidence. Nothing is more damaging to relationships in parishes and communities than breaches of confidence.

Problems in this area can happen easily. You promise to keep something confidential but tell your best friend about it, urging him or her to keep it confidential, too. Your best friend conveys the confidence to someone else—warning them in due course that what they've been told should be considered strictly confidential. And so on. A variant of this chain of broken confidences has to do with conveying confidential information in requests for prayer.

- "I'd like you to keep Earl and his family in your prayers. He told me that his son has just entered rehab."

If that information was told to you in confidence, the fact that you've revealed it in order to garner spiritual support for the person does not eliminate the breach of trust involved.

The only sure way to avoid such problems is to get the person's permission before you reveal something they've told you in confidence.

– "Jane, I realize that what you told me about your mother's condition was told to me in confidence. Would you mind if I let Andrew know? He's so knowledgeable about caregivers in her area."

The great ascetical writer St. John Climacus has some penetrating insights on the spiritual and psychological forces behind a preoccupation with other people's problems:

Hasty and severe judges of the sins of their neighbors fall into this predicament because they have not yet attained to a thorough and constant remembrance of and concern for their own sins. *For if anyone could see his own vices accurately and without the veil of self-love, he would worry about nothing else in this life....*A good grape picker who eats ripe grapes will not start gathering unripe ones. *A charitable and sensible mind takes careful note of whatever virtues it sees in anyone. But a fool looks for faults and defects.* And of such it is said, "They have searched out iniquity and expired in the search."
(St. John Climacus, *Ladder of Divine Ascent*)*

Gossiping *and* listening to gossip are wrong.

An evil doer listens to wicked lips; and a liar gives heed to a mischievous tongue. (Proverbs 17:4)

A Presbyterian pastor in North Carolina once shared how his wife helped him with issues with right speech. When he started to complain about a member of his congregation who annoyed him, his wife interrupted him with "Honey, I love you. But I love Alice, too. Please don't say anything against her to me."

Recently, a friend told me about an incident in a realtor's office, in which the owner of the business began regaling a customer with gossip about a mutual acquaintance. The air was soon thick with toxic assessments of this person. Finally, the realtor's son had had enough. "Will you two cut it out?" he said. "I don't want to hear it."

The conversation abruptly came to a halt and the two perpetrators realized what they had been doing and apologized.

St. John Vianney provides similar advice to those in situations where gossip is being aired:

If something uncharitable is said in your presence, either speak in favor of the [person] absent, or withdraw, or, if possible, stop the conversation.

Gossip affects three people: the person gossiping; the person listening to gossip; and the person being gossiped about. All are harmed. If, for some reason, we cannot avoid listening to gossip, we should decide not to believe or act on what we've heard (it's hearsay), and refrain from repeating it to other people.

One who rejoices in wickedness will be condemned, and for one who hates gossip, evil is lessened. Never repeat a conversation and you will lose nothing at all. *With friend or foe, do not report it, and unless it would be a sin for you, do not disclose it; for someone has heard you and watched you, and when the time comes, he will hate you.* Have you heard a word? Let it die with you. *Be brave! It will not make you burst!* (Sirach 19:5-10)*

Slander or Detraction

Most of us realize that slander is wrong. To slander is to make false charges or accusations against a person or group.

- "Ed must be embezzling money from the parish fund. How else would he be able to afford that month-long cruise?"

However, as in all these areas, there are subtler forms these wrong uses of speech can take. For one thing, it's slander not only when we tell falsehoods about someone, but also when we accuse them of something, or call their integrity into question simply on the basis of personal opinion or attitude.

- "Well, I don't care what anybody thinks, there's something 'fishy' about Peg. I don't know what it is, but something's not right about her."

And then there's negative humor. Negative humor pokes fun at another's weaknesses or faults, mocks sensitivities that person is known to have, or charges the person with some offense, apparently in jest.

43

– "Well, if it isn't our most distinguished parishioner. Nice to see that you find time to associate with the lowly."

Our culture regards negative humor as a legitimate form of kidding, to which the culturally appropriate response is to be a good sport, to show that you don't take yourself too seriously. It's even seen as a backhanded form of affection. Negative humor, also, often masks bad attitudes, jealousy, bitterness and malice, and can take the form of an acceptable way to pass on rumor and gossip without having to take responsibility. Negative humor also often works to undermine the person's self-confidence, however well he or she apparently takes the ribbing. Speaking about oneself in a negative way can also have the same debilitating effect. Saint Francis de Sales wrote: "Slander spoken in a joking way is crueler than all the rest."

Unlearning patterns of negative humor has been a particular difficulty for me. I became a master at it from an early age.. If you want to be one of the boys, a regular guy, this is the way you behave. The only way I've found the wisdom and the courage, over time, to change this aspect of my speech was by being part of a group of brothers and sisters committed to righteousness in this area. This is an important truth: it is a daunting challenge to change a deep habit, a well-established way of speaking and acting, but it's nearly impossible to do so alone. As many sociologists assert, people change in groups.

I saw that point demonstrated vividly on the golf course one day. Three community members showed up to play a round of golf. We asked a guy to join us to make a foursome. As it turned out, our new companion used filthy language as a matter of course, a source of some discomfort and irritation to the rest of us. We said nothing to him and spoke normally, without profanity. By the third hole, his tone had begun to change, and by the fifth hole, he'd dropped the foul language entirely. He picked up on the way we spoke to each other and started following suit. This is the way lasting change in this area happens.

Detraction is the action of disparaging a person or taking away his or her merit or reputation. While detraction might involve slander, that is, making a *false* charge against a person, it also includes making derogatory claims that damage the reputation of another person or group, even when the allegations are true.

This came as a revelation to me when we began to study the area of speech in the community. I knew that I shouldn't go around hurling false or ill-founded charges against people (slander). But I used to think it was perfectly OK to pass on negative information about others provided I knew it was true.

"Did you hear that Joe got fired from his job again? That guy has never managed to learn decent work habits."

"Mary left parish council because her husband says she's neglecting her responsibilities at home."

In Scripture, the word for *slander* is usually the simple phrase: "to speak against"—both in Hebrew and in New Testament Greek. For example, the common Greek term for slander is *katalalia*, literally, "speaking against," as it is used in this passage:

Do not speak against one another, brethren. He who speaks against a brother, or judges a brother, speaks against the law [of God]. (James 4:11)

Note that the biblical term does not distinguish between derogatory statements that are false and those that may be true. We should avoid both slander and detraction.

The Jewish tradition reflects this same understanding. In Chofetz Chaim's famous book *Guard Your Tongue*, he writes:

You are forbidden to relate anything derogatory about others. If a derogatory statement is true, it is termed *loshon hora* (or *lashon hara*, literally "evil speech"). If it is false, even partially so, it is termed *mozti shem ra* ("spreading a bad name") and the offense is much more severe."

In general, we should avoid speaking about others in ways that cause people to think less of that person, or to mistrust them. We should not speak about others in ways that call their righteousness or competence or sincerity into question. On the contrary, our speech should protect and guard other people's reputations, and encourage others to view them and their actions in the best light.

I earnestly exhort you never to slander anyone, either directly or indirectly. Beware of falsely imputing crimes and sins to your neighbor, revealing his secret sins, exaggerating those that are manifest, putting an evil interpretation on his good works, denying the good that you know belongs to someone, maliciously concealing it or lessening it by words. (St. Francis de Sales, *Introduction to the Devout Life*)

Detraction and calumny destroy the reputation and honor of one's neighbor. Honor is the social witness given to human dignity, and *everyone enjoys a natural right to the honor of his name and reputation and to respect.* Thus, detraction and calumny offend against the virtues of justice and charity. (*Catechism of the Catholic Church:* 2479)*

There's a good reason why learning to avoid slander and gossip are the keys to building brotherhood and sisterhood. What sort of relational environment does slander and gossip produce if not one characterized by hostility, quarreling, suspicion, lack of love, and factionalism? If the environment is a religious one, chances are that these bad forms of speech—so habitual in our culture that we hardly even notice them—will be hidden behind a veneer of piety, idealism, and pleasant manners, thus making them even harder to identify and deal with. The Lord wants us to speak about one another in a way that produces a very different sort of relational environment, one characterized by love, respect, and trust, and by speech patterns that bring life and build up the Body of Christ.

In such a supportive environment, people can afford to let their guards down and share deeply; to let brothers and sisters help them with difficulties in their lives; to be real to one another and to God; to risk the challenges of spiritual growth, change, and healing—in short, to let God work. This cannot (and will not) happen if we do not cultivate right speech as a way of life. The trust won't be there. It can't afford to be.

Correction and Forgiveness

This, of course, doesn't mean that one can't voice constructive criticism, or help correct or improve a situation; still less, that one should be silent in the face of clear wrongdoing or fail to prevent someone from inflicting harm. There are ways to address the serious problems that occur in any group while protecting people's reputations and without resorting to the evils of slander and detraction.

The basic principle is modeled on the teaching outlined in Matthew:

If your brother sins against you, go and tell him his fault, between you and him alone. *If he listens to you, you have gained your brother.* (Matthew 18:15)*

You will note that this this approach is characterized by dealing directly with the person you believe has wronged you. By contrast, our society trains us to deal with difficulties indirectly: If I don't like what someone is doing—withdraw affection; refuse to speak to them; talk to everyone in sight about what he or she has done—*except the person*. What the Lord wants is for us to go directly to the person involved and deal with the problem face to face.

The passage goes on to sketch out a kind of judicial process involving witnesses and appeal to church leaders. The essential point, however, is that when dealing with perceived or suspected wrongdoing on someone's part, *go first to the person involved and discuss it with that person privately.*

While other steps may be involved in order to resolve the problem, this approach allows wrongdoing or grievances to be confronted directly, but discreetly, protecting people's reputations. This approach also prevents the issue—which may, in the end, involve only two people or a small group—from becoming a matter of public discussion.

Even in the course of opposing error or resolving disagreements, the Christian approach is to avoid rash judgments and to correct with patience and gentleness:

> Every good Christian ought to be more ready to give a favorable interpretation to another's statement than to condemn it. But if he cannot do so, let him ask how the other understands it. And if the latter understands it badly, let the former correct him with love. If that does not suffice, let the Christian try all suitable ways to bring the other to a correct interpretation so that he may be saved. (Ignatius of Loyola, *Spiritual Exercises*, 22)

If we have slandered someone, we must make *appropriate reparation—that is, repair the damage.* It's not enough simply to catch oneself after slandering someone or betraying a confidence and say to oneself: "Oh, gosh, I guess I shouldn't have done that."

As the *Catechism* notes:

> Every offense committed against justice and truth entails the duty of reparation, even if its author has been forgiven....This duty of reparation also concerns offenses against another's reputation. This reparation, moral and sometimes material, must be evaluated in terms of the extent of the damage inflicted. It obliges in conscience. (*Catechism of the Catholic Church:* 2487)

One must clearly repent of having slandered someone, but, if possible, one should also ask forgiveness of the person or persons we have slandered—in effect, to make restitution to the person whose reputation has been hurt.

–"Fred, I said things about you I had no business saying. This is what I said ___. It was wrong of me to say it. I'll never do it again. I ask your forgiveness."

In addition, we need to go to the people who heard our slander, and, whenever possible, unsay it.

– "I had no business telling you ____. It's not true. Please forgive me."

Obviously, as the *Catechism* observes, we need to be sensible (and realistic) in the way we make restitution for sins of the tongue. It may not always be possible to address these matters by going to the persons involved—although, in my experience, the keen embarrassment involved in having to do so is one of the single most effective ways to ensure that we avoid slander and gossip in the future.

Speech and Love

As with everything in Christian life, it all starts, not with rules and regulations, but with the heart. In an earlier verse of the passage quoted above, Jesus declares:

"Out of the abundance of the heart, the mouth speaks." (Matthew 12:34b)

Righteous speech is not simply an external matter of saying the right things and avoiding those that are harmful, still less a matter of being a little nicer to people. It's a matter of the redemption of our inner life—first, the commitment of the heart to God's will, to the vision of the new man which the Spirit wishes to form in us. It will do no good to memorize a bunch of rules about proper speech if we're not first ready to be instruments of God's mercy and love in the world, seeking to be docile to the work of His Spirit.

As the apostle writes in the passage quoted above:

Be renewed in the spirit of your minds, *and put on the new nature, created after the likeness of God, in true righteousness and holiness.* (Ephesians 4:23-24)

As with everything else in life, the decision to make real changes in behavior—in this case, in the area of speech—takes place in the depths of the heart.

In its most practical sense, the whole area of right speech takes place in the realm of our thoughts, with the character of our thought life. Gossip and slander begin in our minds long before our lips utter them.

We can't really, therefore, master the world of speech until we deal with the tendency to judgment with which our minds are filled.

Part of the fundamental decision we are required to make has to do with whether we choose to be our brother or sister's advocate, or his or her accuser. In Scripture, the Holy Spirit is called the "Advocate"—the "defense" (John 14:16ff)—in other words, the one who pleads the cause of another, while Satan is described, in this judicial metaphor, as the "accuser"—in effect, the prosecuting attorney. (Job 1:9-11; Revelation 12:10)

The actions of the Holy Spirit build up the person—equip, hearten, and defend him—in short, create the new man. The actions of the accuser tear him down.

The call of right speech demands that we adopt the position, not only in words but in thoughts, of our brother or sister's advocate—the one who appeals to their best instincts, who believes in the power of God's call in their lives, rather than the position of the accuser—the one who, with exquisite critical acumen, builds the case for their condemnation.

As one of my mentors, Father Charles Harris, has sagely observed:

We all tend to set up our little judgment seats and everyone we know passes before those judgment seats in spite of the warning of our Lord: "Judge not, that you not be judged."

Virtue grows in us under the influence of kindly thoughts, just as viciousness develops into rash judgment. We often find ourselves violently tempted to the sins we have been attributing to others, and the harsh thoughts are like seeds ready to sprout into evil. In a very real sense, we are what we think, and from our thoughts spring words. In the end, the effort to redeem our speech is merely a feature of the call to love. As we are called to love our neighbor with our resources, we are called to love him or her with our speech, too. We cannot say that we love our neighbor in our hearts, while despising him in our thoughts or belittling him with our words. It's not an easy transformation, to be sure, but it is an essential one.

We have to acknowledge that we are living in a gossip-slander-and-

49

detraction-driven society, in which there are increasingly few constraints of any kind on speech. This fact means that we have a doubly high hill to climb in appropriating the norms of godly speech:

1. The social environment in which we live works against our aims.
2. The popular tabloid-saturated culture has given us an appetite for many of the negative forms of speech we will need to (gradually) unlearn.

This is why it's so important to be making these changes as part of a group effort. As a group or community, we can help each other develop both sides of the speech equation—not merely unlearning destructive patterns, but, more importantly, learning, with patience and the grace of God, the life-giving speech of the kingdom.

Things to Think and Pray About

Taking the call to righteous speech seriously is the essential first step to the practical application of the call to love. Let's ask the Holy Spirit to open us up to the will of God in each area of our lives and to help us overcome the inner resistance that can arise in any of us to the life-giving ways He wishes to teach us.

- Right speech begins with the heart.
- Right speech depends on the character of our thought life. Right speech is a creature of mercy and kindness and involves putting away judgmental attitudes.
- The speech of the kingdom is a speech that seeks to serve.
- The Lord wants us to speak about one another in a way that produces trust, respect, and love.
- In the way that I speak to and about others, am I my brother or sister's advocate (Holy Spirit) or his or her prosecuting attorney (Satan)?

Chapter 4
Gratitude

And let the peace of Christ rule in your hearts, to which indeed you were called in the one body. And be thankful.

Colossians 3:15

Gratitude is not only the greatest of the virtues but it is also the parent of them all.

Cicero

Some years ago, a friend told me about a life-changing experience he'd had. Faced with the needs of an ailing parent, he had made some serious adjustments in his life: he had reduced his workload and moved back to the family home located in a small town. Although these decisions were made freely, out of a sense of his responsibilities as a son, he found himself increasingly unhappy with the way his life had turned out. In a word, he felt trapped—trapped by his sense of filial duty, and by the limitations, as he saw them, of the lifestyle to which that sense of duty confined him.

In the midst of these unhappy reflections, he heard the Lord tell him that the secret to his life—and to a renewal of his sense of purpose—was gratitude. He needed to open his heart to the realities of his own life, as they were, and to the goodness and opportunities God had placed there, and to stop regretting the choices he had made or the fact that he had not been given some other kind of life.

It was a key moment for him. Over time, he found himself able to embrace his life more fully, with its challenges, and in doing so, discovered the many blessings he had been unable to see before, the many opportunities for life and growth to which his resentment and anger had blinded him. Afterward, he often encouraged others with the notion that one will never see one's life for what it really is until one is prepared to be *grateful* for it.

The biblical notion of gratitude, echoed in my friend's story, is a very large concept, indeed—one that is central to building Christian brotherhood and sisterhood as well as to inspiring a personal vision of life. There is a great deal more involved with gratitude, in the sense that we're using it, than simply being a bit more thoughtful, or saying thank you more often—although, as we'll see, these common forms of gratitude are part of it.

Gratitude is a whole approach to life, a whole way of relating to God and

51

neighbor. It's deeply personal, as in being a grateful person, but it is more than that. Gratitude is meant to be part of the way people live, the culture of a grateful people. **So, in its essence, gratitude is an attitude, a behavior, and a culture.**

What Is Gratitude?

Let's call on one of the psalms, Psalm 116, which is often called a psalm of gratitude, to help us.

> *I love the Lord, because he has heard my voice and my supplications.*
> *Because he inclined his ear to me, therefore I will call on him as long as I live. The snares of death encompassed me; the pangs of Sheol laid hold on me;*
> *I suffered distress and anguish.*
> *Then I called on the name of the Lord:*
> *"O Lord, I beseech thee, save my life!"*
> *Gracious is the Lord and righteous; our God is merciful.*
> *The Lord preserves the simple;*
> *when I was brought low, he saved me.*
> *Return, O my soul, to your rest; for the Lord has dealt bountifully with you...*
> *What shall I render to the Lord for all his bounty to me?*
> *I will lift up the cup of salvation and call on the name of the Lord,*
> *I will pay my vows to the Lord in the presence of all his people.*
> (Psalm 116:1-14)

The first verses (1-4) describe the character of the situation, possibly the Babylonian captivity (6th century BC), when many of the leaders of the Jewish people were deported to Babylon. (For the background, see Jeremiah chapter 52.)

What does the Psalmist do in this crisis? He turns to God. He calls on the name of the Lord. The motive behind the Psalmist's prayer is that he *remembers* what God has done in the past; he recalls the *character of God*. God's response to the Psalmist's plight: He saves him from the mortal threats he faces.

Now comes the important part (for our purposes): "What shall I render to the Lord for all his bounty to me?" (verse 12). The Psalmist asks a question: How am I to show gratitude to the Lord in return for His favors to me?

The next verses (12-14) provide the answer:

1. *I will lift up the cup of salvation:* Literally, I will thank (or exalt) God for the ways He has saved me (the "cup of salvation").
2. *I will call on the name of the Lord*: I will let Him work in my life more and more, trusting in His graciousness.
3. *I will pay my vows to the Lord in the presence of all his people*: I will live out my gratitude publicly so that others may put their trust in God.

Using the framework of this psalm, then, as a source for the definition of gratitude, we see what gratitude is. As Psalm 116 lays it out, then, we can already see that gratitude is a great deal more than good manners. It is a whole spiritual outlook, a way of life. What's more, a Catholic will need little prompting to see in the psalm's approach its solid Eucharistic lines, theology that will find its full articulation in the actions and language of the Eucharistic Prayers of the Mass.

Since gratitude in this biblical sense is such a large and embracing concept, there is no single biblical term for it. (We saw the same thing with the biblical notion of mercy.) Gratitude undergirds the whole relationship of God and His people and His people's relations with each other. Let's look at two sets of biblical words for gratitude under the headings **gift** and **thanksgiving**.

Gift (Grace)

Look at some of the different ways we can think about the word *gift*.

Favor

I will make all my goodness pass before you, and will proclaim before you my Name, the Lord; I will be gracious to whom I will be gracious and I will show mercy to whom I will show mercy. (Exodus 33:19)

Favor is a matter of free choice. God's choice (favor) is based on His own goodness, not necessarily on the merits of the receiver. Favor is essentially an **unmerited gift.** In the New Testament, Jesus tells us that we are to show favor (grace, graciousness, consideration, kindness), even to those who have sinned against us, or who persecute us, precisely because God's unmerited favor has been shown to us (see Luke 10:29-37). This, of course, as we have seen, is the basis of covenant love.

Grace

For the wages of sin is death, but the free gift of God is eternal life in Christ

Jesus our Lord. (Romans 6:23)*

God sent His Son to die in order that we might have eternal life. This is the greatest possible favor that we could receive—this, while we were still the enemies of God and His plan. (Romans 5:6-17) God's free gift is eternal life, the ultimate sign of the gracious character of God and the depth of His love.

Charism

Now there are varieties of gifts [charisms], but the same Spirit; and there are varieties of service, but the same Lord; and there are varieties of working, but it is the same God who inspires them all in every one. To each is given the manifestation of the Spirit for the common good...All these are inspired by one and the same Spirit, who apportions to each one individually as he wills. (I Corinthians 12:4-7, 11)

Charisms—a word that has become familiar to Catholics, if not through Scripture study, then through the term "charismatic renewal"—refers to the free gifts that the Holy Spirit gives to equip the Church—spiritual gifts that are given "to each one individually, as he [the Spirit] wills." The chapter goes on to list them (verses 8-10). These gifts or charisms are given, not to privileged individuals, but to build up the Body of Christ, to empower the Church. No one auditions for these gifts; no one can earn or deserve them, the apostle stresses; the Holy Spirit gives them freely.

Eucharist (Thanksgiving)

The second major set of biblical words dealing with gratitude has to do with the response to the graciousness of God. The Greek word *eucharistein*, which we know from its identification with the Mass, has a broader application in Scripture as a word meaning "to give thanks, or to praise."

Jesus Himself is our model of the Eucharistic personality, whose response to God's action in His and others' lives is *praise*. In fact, the Gospels indicate that praise is a fundamental element in Jesus' relationship with His Father.

1. When the disciples of Jesus return, flushed with success, from their first apostolic mission, how does Jesus respond?

In that same hour, he rejoiced in the Holy Spirit and said, "I thank thee, Father, Lord of heaven and earth, that thou hast hidden these things from the *wise and understanding and revealed them to babes; yea, Father, for such was thy gracious will."* (Luke 10:21)*

2.   Before the raising of Lazarus, Jesus prays:

And Jesus lifted up his eyes and said, "Father, I thank thee *that thou hast heard me. I knew that thou hearest me always but I have said this on account of the people standing by, that they may believe that thou didst send me."* (John 11:41b-42)*

The New Testament epistles, echoing this pattern, urge that Christian life, speech, and culture be characterized by the wisdom of thanksgiving as the Lord's was:

Look carefully how you walk [conduct yourselves], *not as unwise men, but as wise, making the most of the time, because the days are evil. Therefore, do not be foolish, but understand what the will of the Lord is. And do not get drunk with wine, for that is debauchery, but* be filled with the Spirit, addressing one another in psalms and hymns and spiritual songs, singing and making melody to the Lord with all your heart, always and for everything giving thanks in the name of our Lord Jesus Christ to God the Father. (Ephesians 5:15-20)*

There is a similar list in First Thessalonians:

See that none of you repays evil for evil, but always seek to do good to one another and to all. Rejoice always, pray constantly, give thanks in all circumstances; for this is the will of God in Christ Jesus for you.
(I Thessalonians 5:15-18)

The motivation for this thanksgiving (echoing Exodus 19:6) is spelled out in First Peter:
But you are a chosen race, a royal priesthood, a holy nation, God's own people, that you may declare the wonderful deeds of him *who called you out of darkness into his marvelous light. Once you were no people but now you are God's people; once you had not received mercy but now you have received mercy.* (I Peter 2:9-10)*

Three things are worth emphasizing here as we seek to grasp the vision of gratitude in these biblical passages.

1. **The idea of thanksgiving as a way of life contrasts with many cultural attitudes today.** Part of the problem has to do with the observation we've made before: that our culture tends to be focused on function rather than on relationship. We thank people if and when they've done something for us, and we refrain from thanking them when they fail to perform according to our expectations. It doesn't take much insight to notice the self-referential character of this approach, or the problem it poses to our appreciation of the character of our relationship to God.

   Thanking God and thanking others only when they manage to give me what I want, or think I want, is short-sighted, to say the least.

   I once knew a parishioner who was routinely enthused whenever his prayers for short-term financial help were answered, but grew indignant with God—and threatened to withdraw belief in Him!—whenever his perceived emergencies were not met with miracles.

   The Eucharistic relationship into which God wishes to lead us has to do with the character of our whole lives, not the exigencies of the moment.

2. The second point to ponder is more mystical. I remember a discussion some years ago with a Catholic convert who found herself confused by the predominant note of praise in Catholic worship. "I just don't understand why God needs all that praise? Is He insecure or something?" she asked.

   Trying to find a way to orient her, I said that praise and thanksgiving are necessary to us, not to God. He does not need our praise. It is we who need the language of praise and thanksgiving to prepare us for the life of heaven.

   The language of heaven, as we see it mirrored in the images of Scripture, is a language of praise. To say that it is a language of praise is to say that it is a language of reality. As we noted earlier, to be grateful and to give thanks is simply to acknowledge the real world, to see our lives for what they really are—utterly dependent on the grace of God and the goodwill and care of others.

   In addition, the habit of thanksgiving acquaints and trains us in the native language of the angels and the saints. That such training can seem onerous or, worse, artificial to us only makes sense. Since our expulsion from Eden, the human race has studiously cultivated languages rich with complaint, recrimination, and blasphemy—a dark and bitter speech we will have to unlearn if we wish to have access to our true homeland, heaven.

Worship, in this sense, is both an aspect of our relationship to God—we owe Him worship because of who He is—and basic training for life with Him, the life of heaven for which human beings were created. In that sense, we become ourselves most fully when we praise God.

> *Then I looked, and I heard around the throne and the living creatures and the elders the voice of many angels, numbering myriads of myriads and thousands of thousands, saying with a loud voice, "Worthy is the Lamb who was slain, to receive power and wealth and wisdom and might and honor and glory and blessing!" And I heard every creature in heaven and on earth and under the earth and in the sea and all therein saying, "To him who sits upon the throne and to the Lamb be blessing and honor and glory and might for ever and ever!" And the four living creatures said, "Amen!" and the elders fell down and worshiped.* (Revelation 5:11-14)

3. Most importantly, gratitude is both the content and the motivation of our fundamental relationship to God.

Once we realize the truth of who God is, and who we are, and begin to grasp the depth of His love for us, our whole lives become an act of gratitude to God for all He has done, all He is doing, and all He will do for us. When we become part of God's people, we become a people whose very life, meaning, and purpose is *gratitude, thanksgiving, and praise.* This brings us home to covenant, again: **gratitude is our covenant response to the graciousness of the covenant-keeping God.** As the Psalmist pointed out at the beginning of our discussion, trusting in the Lord when faced with difficult, or even dire circumstances, believing in, and acting on His graciousness even when it is not apparent or visible to us in the circumstances is part of covenant loyalty.

How Do We Show Gratitude to God?

We can never repay the Lord fully or adequately for His goodness to us. Our gratitude will always be unequal to His gift. Nevertheless, there are fundamental attitudes and practices we can adopt which help us respond to the Lord's kindness.

Meditation

One of the key elements in gratitude is awareness of the goodness shown to us. Opening ourselves to the Lord's goodness in our lives, becoming conscious of these realities should be an everyday part of our prayer and thought life. Here is a list of things that you can thank God for:

■ **The gift of life**, of existence itself

■ **The greatness of or benefit of our bodies**, "so fearfully and wonderfully made," as Scripture says (Psalm 139:13-15)

■ **The benefit of our minds, senses, and other faculties**—for the great being that we are

■ **The universe** created for us that we might know, love, and serve God

■ **The Scriptures and the Tradition of the Church**, for the revelation of the truth

■ **Christian life, our salvation, the Sacraments**, for all the means given to us in order that we might live in the light of the Lord Jesus

In a similar vein, here is a list of issues to consider in a daily examination of conscience:

■ Our tendency to **rebel** against God and neglect His commands

■ Our **reluctance** to embrace the truth, to understand and appropriate the Gospel

■ The **little diligence** we have shown in His service—especially in the light of all the gifts He has given us

■ The **barriers** we put up in our lives to defend ourselves against the call of love

Regular reflection on such questions can help dispose us to open our hearts to gratitude.

Devotion

The Latin word *devotum* means "to set apart, to dedicate, to give away wholly." Devotion has to do with making a decision, deep in our hearts, to live for God, to offer our whole lives to His worship, service, and glory. Such a decision, of course, is not made once but renewed daily. It is a facet of what we might call a "covenant exchange": God gives all to me; as a response, I give my all to Him.

Saint Ignatius of Loyola's *Spiritual Exercises* concludes his *Contemplation to Attain the Love of God* with this famous prayer, which perfectly expresses the sense of this decision:

Take, Lord, receive all my liberty, my memory, my understanding, and my entire will, all that I have and possess. Thou hast given all to me. To Thee, O Lord, I return it. All is Thine, dispose of it wholly according to Thy will. Give me Thy love and Thy grace, for this is sufficient for me.

Service
"I am among you as one who serves." (Luke 22:27)

Service involves coming before the Lord and beseeching Him to use us in the furtherance of His plan. More than a heartfelt prayer, service involves positioning our lives in a practical sense so that God can employ us in His work, and in the particular mission He has chosen for us. Readiness to be used by the Lord is an expression of gratitude.

Needless to say, beseeching the Lord to use us is a serious business. We can hardly go about making practical decisions about where we live or what professions or job opportunities we'll pursue without taking God's will and the good of His Church and the good of those He's placed us with into consideration.

A caveat here: our motivation in serving the Lord is an important consideration. Being generous or self-sacrificing out of a wrong motivation—the praise of others, group pressure from friends and associates, heroic or romantic images of oneself—can lead to serious difficulties later on, to a structural weakness in the nature of one's commitments. As the Lord Himself warns in one of His most challenging admonitions, if we do all that we're called to do, "we are unprofitable servants. We have only done our duty." (Luke 17:10)

No godly project, spiritual aim, or ministry can be built, or prosper, without gratitude. Gratitude constitutes the eyes of the soul—perceiving the world as it really is—and making its response on that basis. Without gratitude, we're flying blind.

The next three fundamentals of gratitude are not attitudes as such, but practices—different ways of making Meditation, Devotion, and Service concrete in everyday life.

Piety

Like the word *duty, piety* is something of a dirty word in today's world. For many people, *piety* conjures up notions of strictness and rigidity. However, like duty, it's a perfectly good word that refers to a very important aspect of faith that tends to get neglected these days. Given our culture's individualistic orientation and focus on spontaneity and emotional engagement, it's easy for us to dismiss traditional spiritual practices—the practices of piety—as unnecessary or outdated in favor of a purely interior, subjective faith. But that would be a mistake. As humans, our faith needs physical concrete expression and preferably ones we don't have to improvise on the spot. Our Catholic tradition provides us with many helpful, time-tested ways to express our faith. These become, then, external signs, incarnations of what is in our hearts.

These might include: a daily examination of conscience; setting aside particular times of day to pray and reflect on Scripture (*e.g.,* the Liturgy of the Hours; saying blessings on arising from sleep and before going to bed at night, and at meals). Physical gestures can also be helpful in expressing gratitude to God in prayer: prostration (submission to God's will); kneeling (pledging fealty to God); raising hands (prayer with confidence of victory). Such gestures as these, along with others you may find helpful, express in concrete terms the greatness and goodness of God and His gifts and our response to Him.

Needless to say, the greatest single way we express our gratitude to God in prayer is through our celebration of the Eucharist.

> The Eucharist is the source and summit of the Christian life...For in the Eucharist is contained the whole spiritual good of the Church, namely Christ himself, our Pasch. (*Catechism of the Catholic Church:* 1324)

Sacrifices

This involves devoting things in our lives to the service of God—dedicating our time to the service of a neighbor (good deeds); praying in a special way for someone in need; fasting and almsgiving; all manner of good deeds done out of reverence for the Lord. As the Book of Tobit notes:

> *Then the angel...said to them: "Praise God and give thanks to him; exalt him and give thanks to him in the presence of all the living for what he has done for you. It is good to praise God and to exalt his name, worthily declaring the works of God. Do not be slow to give him thanks....Prayer is good when accompanied by fasting, almsgiving, and righteousness....Those who perform*

deeds of charity and righteousness will have fullness of life. (Tobit 12:6-9)*

Oblations

While connected to the previous category of sacrificial good deeds, oblations refers in a particular way to dedicating material resources to God's use—specifically for the furthering of God's plan in the world, for the work of the Church. This might include giving money for missions, helping a poor rural parish rebuild after a fire, providing for the poor at Christmas, or even the sacrifice of a livelihood to do lay missionary work for a few years.

Psalm 22 provides a good illustration of this process at work:

I will tell of thy name to my brethren;
In the midst of the congregation I will praise thee:
You who fear the Lord, praise him!
For he has not despised or abhorred the affliction of the afflicted.
From thee comes my praise in the great congregation;
My vows I will pay before those who fear him.
The afflicted shall eat and be satisfied;
Those who seek him shall praise the Lord!
*(Psalm 22:22-26)**

The Psalmist publicly declares the saving help of the Lord. As a response to what God has done, the Psalmist makes a public vow—that is, he dedicates his life more fully to God, pledging that he will translate his thanksgiving into good deeds and a righteous life. As a result of his response to God, "the afflicted shall eat"—needs are met, the poor have goodness shown to them, and they, in turn, seek the Lord. Thus we have the biblical pattern of gratitude: remembrance, trust, and service—the goodness of God reverberating in the community through gratitude.

Gratitude in Relations to Others

The pattern of gratitude we've seen in relation to God also applies to other relationships.

We owe a special and unique debt of gratitude to our parents. There is a reason why the Ten Commandments place honoring parents, as the first of the social commandments, directly after those concerning our relationship to God. After God, our parents are the cause of every good that we possess—including life itself. They not only gave us life in the first place, but they sustained us in life when, as children, we would have been incapable of sustaining ourselves. (This, of course, includes adoptive parents, who have also sustained us in life.) Beyond any personal qualities, gifts, and resources our parents brought to their responsibilities, this alone—life and basic sustenance—would be enough to motivate our gratitude—a debt, like the debt of gratitude owed to God that we can never hope to fully repay. If training in the ways of the Lord and a godly life are added to that, parents have truly been vehicles of the Lord's own love and care for us.

Honor your father and your mother, that your days may be long in the land which the Lord your God gives you. (Exodus 20:12)

Deuteronomy has a somewhat longer version of the commandment:

Honor your father and your mother, as the Lord your God commanded you; that your days may be prolonged, and that it may go well with you in the land which the Lord your God gives you. (Deuteronomy 5:16)

We'll discuss honoring parents more fully in the next chapter. Suffice to say here that our basic debt to parents can be summarized under two headings: respect and service.

Respect

Respect for parents (filial piety) derives from gratitude toward those who, by the gift of life, their love and their work, have brought children into the world and enabled them to grow in stature, wisdom, and grace. "With all your heart honor your father, and do not forget the birth pangs of your mother. Remember that through your parents you were born; what can you give back to them that equals their gift to you?" (Sirach 7:27-28) (*Catechism of the Catholic Church:* 2215)

When younger, respect for parents on the part of children involves active docility and obedience to "all that [parents] ask of him when it is for his good, or that of the family." (*Catechism of the Catholic Church:* 2217)

Later on, that obedience is tempered, as children grow older. Still, respect continues.

As they grow up, children should continue to respect their parents. They should anticipate their wishes, willingly seek their advice, and accept their just admonitions. Obedience to parents ceases with the emancipation of the children; not so respect, which is always owed to them. This respect has its roots in the fear of God, one of the gifts of the Holy Spirit. (*Catechism of the Catholic Church:* 2217)

Service

The Hebrew term for *honor*—as in "honor your father and mother"—implies not only respect, but also **material, financial obligations, along with personal service**. This indicates that the practical implications of gratitude to parents grows, not lessens with time.

By now we should be familiar with the gratitude equation. If parents provided you with life and sustenance when you were young and vulnerable, gratitude means that you must provide them with life and sustenance, or ensure that sustenance when they are old and infirm. This honor involves not only financial help, if it is needed, but direct personal service and care as well. As the *Catechism* teaches:

The fourth commandment reminds grown children of their responsibilities toward their parents. As much as they can, they must give them material and moral support in old age and in times of illness, loneliness, or distress. Jesus recalls this duty of gratitude. (Mark 7:10-12) (*Catechism of the Catholic Church:* 2218)

Or, as the Book of Sirach, which links gratitude to God with filial piety, reminds us:

For the Lord honored the father above the children, and he confirmed the right of the mother over her sons. Whoever honors his father atones for sins, and whoever glorifies his mother is like one who lays up treasure. Whoever honors his father will be gladdened by his own children, and when he prays he will be heard. Whoever glorifies his father will have long life, and whoever obeys the Lord will refresh his mother. (Sirach 3:2-6)

One cannot miss the point here that gratitude in the biblical sense is linked to the notion of debt. If someone does good to us, we are in debt to them and, by implication, committed to returning the favor—in effect, to ensuring that goodness is passed on and increased in the community. Missing from the biblical equation is the idea that gratitude is linked to whether or not we especially like the person to whom we're indebted, or whether we enjoy an especially close bond with them. Gratitude is linked to the relationship. One can be a deeply grateful son without necessarily being best buddies with your dad. Obviously, it's a plus and a boon if the relationship and the warm bond go together, but the gratitude is still there even if that's not the case.

Our Debt of Gratitude to Those Who Do Us a Favor

We owe a debt of gratitude to anyone who freely does us a favor—

- Who honors us
- Who chooses to loan or give us money
- Who gives us gifts
- Who cares for our lives
- Who shows concern
- Who prays for us

What we have to understand is that when people do good to us, this act expresses (or establishes) a *relationship.* Respect, honor, and loyalty go with the transaction.

For example, a brother comes to you, someone you know, and says: "I hear you're in some financial difficulty. Can I help?" Should you accept his offer of a loan or an outright gift, he becomes your *benefactor;* the two of you enter into a special relationship linked to his freely given gift. He is, in effect, supporting or subsidizing some part of your life; he is enabling you to feed your family, or provide for your parents, or pay your taxes.

If all goes well, there can be genuine growth in love and respect between the parties, and others who see a successful outcome might be encouraged to be generous. However, if the recipient fails to pay back the loan, or abuses or takes advantage of his benefactor's kindness, mistrust and division are the likely result —a failure that will leave a bad taste in everyone's mouth and cause others to think twice about helping people out.

When you take out a personal loan, money is not the only thing involved; you take out a loan on the relationship, too. Scripture is quite realistic on this point:

He that shows mercy will lend to his neighbor, and he that strengthens him with his hand keeps the commandments. Lend to your neighbor in the time of his need; and, in turn, repay your neighbor promptly. Confirm your word and keep faith with him, and on every occasion you will find what you need. Many persons regard a loan as a windfall, and cause trouble to those who help them. A man will kiss another's hands until he gets a loan, and will lower his voice in speaking of his neighbor's money, but at the time for repayment he will delay, and will pay in words of unconcern, and will find fault with the time....The borrower has robbed him of his money and he has needlessly made him his enemy....Because of such wickedness, therefore, many have refused to lend; they have been afraid of being defrauded needlessly. (Sirach 29:1-7)

In general, when someone does a favor or something good for us, there are many ways we can repay him or her, or return the favor:

- We can praise or thank them publicly.
- We can perform personal services: mowing the lawn, trimming trees, babysitting.
- We can send cards, flowers, or other gifts for special occasions, anniversaries, birthdays.
- If a person has a material need, we can meet it, or organize a group effort to address it.
- We can spend time with them; make a gift; give music lessons to their children; provide them with information or advice about an issue with which they're concerned.

Remember that repayment should not be done anxiously or with a desire simply to get rid of the obligation. The culture of gratitude is about good deeds inspiring generous responses—about creating an environment, not of legalistic tit for tat but of abounding goodness and thanksgiving.

As Jesus Himself teaches in Luke's version of the Sermon on the Mount: *"Give, and it will be given to you; good measure, pressed down, shaken together, running over, will be put into your lap. For the measure you give, will be the measure you get back."* (Luke 6:38)

Ingratitude

But understand this, that in the last days there will come times of stress. For men will be lovers of self, lovers of money, proud, arrogant, abusive, disobe-

dient to their parents, ungrateful, *unholy, inhuman, implacable, slanderers, profligates, fierce, haters of good, treacherous, reckless, swollen with conceit, lovers of pleasure rather than lovers of God, holding the form of religion but denying the power of it.* (2 Timothy 3:1-5)*

It's sobering to find ingratitude among the identifying marks of the worldly man, the false brother in this thoroughly hair-raising passage. It's clear, not only from the New Testament, but from the Old Testament's denunciations of murmuring and grumbling that ingratitude occupies a privileged place in the list of obstacles to God and the workings of grace.

Ingratitude can be expressed in many ways: We can routinely notice but fail to express gratitude for what people do for us; we can fail to appreciate the favor being shown; and, worse yet, we can even fail to notice when people are being kind to us. This is why Scripture describes ingratitude not only as a serious character flaw, but as a form of spiritual blindness.

Part of our spiritual resistance to the notion that we should pay attention to the good people do to us—that we should live as fundamentally grateful persons—has to do, I think, with the arrogance built into our culture's ideal of the autonomous individual.

A high school friend, when asked what he wanted to be when he grew up, said: "I want to be someone who never needs any one, who never has to depend on other people."

I remember being struck at the time by the isolation and despair such a sentiment revealed. But many of us have been affected by such attitudes buried in the assumptions of our culture. **If we're required to borrow money, or we're the recipients of some other favor, a common cultural response is shame**. We're embarrassed by our needs in part because we assume that we should be completely self-sufficient, beholden to no one. Often, we're even secretly resentful of our benefactors and those who try to help and the inferior social position to which our needs—so we imagine—have reduced us.

Ingratitude takes root in such soil. But, as we've seen, such a notion—that we should never be obligated or beholden to anyone—is pure illusion. **We are born beholden—to God, to our parents, to our ancestors, to nursing staff, to the myriads of people who have created the conditions for our life and survival** and we continue in that radical need for others until the day we draw our last breath—and beyond.

Learning to receive is a key aspect of Christian life. In most cases, receiving is much more difficult than giving, but both giving and receiving are not only part of life, but essential spiritual arts.

Reality consists in opening our eyes to the good God showers upon us, minute by minute, both directly, and through the love and care of the people He has placed in our lives.

Imagination and Love

Three last comments:

Firstly, gratitude, in the biblical sense, focuses on *deeds*—particularly deeds as the defining element in determining character. We know the character of God because we remember His deeds; we recall His saving *acts*. We trust Him because we know what He has *done* for us. While we know that God loves us, we know the character, the depth of that love, not from mystical intuition into the inner workings of His emotional life, but, ultimately, from the character of the sacrifice of Jesus—God's willingness to deliver His own son to death for our salvation.

This same perception applies to our attitudes toward the good and kindly deeds of others. It is all too common for contemporary men and women to insist on knowing whether someone who does a good deed really means it. This, of course, is yet another example of the primacy of emotions in our culture, and the way we privilege emotions in determining whether someone or some act is authentic. As we accept that the deeds of God disclose His character, we also accept that the good deeds of our brothers and sisters similarly manifest the character of their love.

The thank you card sent by someone who is a committed brother or sister in your parish means what it says—that people love and appreciate you. It may not be exciting in the emotional sense—but it is real.

This, of course, does not mean that good deeds are to be performed in a routine or offhand way. But what it does point to is that in living a life of thanksgiving, we must look to deeds—not speculations about inner dispositions—to determine the character of love.

Secondly, learning to be grateful is a whole approach to life. Learning that approach is a process—it's an art, something that one grows into, that one gets better at over time.

While gratitude certainly involves changes in personal attitudes, it's not just a personal or individual affair. When we're talking about gratitude, we're talking about something big, about human nature as it was (and is) supposed to be. Ideally, gratitude is part of normal human culture, something learned as a child, a natural part of what it means to be human. That contemporary human society in many instances has lost contact with these values is tragic, but we can neither accept the status quo, nor go with the times and rationalize the loss.

Since the culture of gratitude is essential to human and spiritual life, we have no choice but to become part of a process to restore it. Gratitude is part of the life we're meant to have—both as human beings and as Christians.

Clearly, such a restoration is a matter of grace. We will need God's help and enlightenment in order to do this. But it's also a matter of trial and error on our part, involving careful, prudent attempts to revive a culture of gratitude in our own lives and communities. It will also involve enlisting what might be called the insights of the moral imagination—putting on the mind of Christ.

Which brings me to the last point—It's often occurred to me that when it comes to the daily work of loving people, we can tend to be both perfunctory and unimaginative in the way we go about it.

We all know people who put a great deal of thought and prayer into the ways they show kindness to others. But, in my experience, that's hardly the rule. That's especially the case when we're confronted with difficulties and with difficult people.

If we're faced with a difficult person or a situation we don't know how to handle, the response is often—at least my response is often to throw up my hands and either ignore the situation or put off confronting it as long as possible. In fact, what I think we're called to do is to pray for the Lord's guidance and to use our imaginations.

Isn't it strange that, as a Christian people, we've spent centuries using our imaginations to paint icons, build cathedrals, and create music to express our faith, but rarely use that same imaginative capacity to love other people, to extend and enhance Christian moral culture?

Love and gratitude are not just about principles and demands. They're also about imagination and creativity.

Things to Think and Pray About

Gratitude is to recognize and celebrate the real world in which we are the recipients of innumerable gifts from God, whatever our specific circumstances. Out of gratitude, we create an environment of goodness that translates into good deeds, service, and devotion. But consistent effort is required to overcome the obstacles, self-sufficiency, sense of entitlement, resentments and negativity, that all too frequently block the path to grati-

tude.

- "Gratitude is not only the greatest of the virtues, but it is also the parent of them all." (Cicero)
- We need to understand that we own nothing. Everything we have is a gift from God.
- How do we consume our two great tangible resources—time and money? Whom do they serve?
- "Jesus does not look for great deeds, but only for gratitude and self-surrender." (St. Therese of Lisieux)
- We become ourselves most fully when we praise God.
- If the only prayer you say in your life is 'thank you,' that would suffice. (Meister Eckhart)

Chapter 5
Honor

Let love be genuine; hate what is evil, hold fast to what is good; love one another with brotherly affection; outdo one another in showing honor.

Romans 12:9–10

Honor is the social witness given to human dignity.

Catechism of the Catholic Church (2479)

Honor is a word that has a faintly old-fashioned ring. It's still used in our society, but largely as a vestige of older terminology and forms of address:

– "Yes, your honor."
– "We request the honor of your presence."
– "She's been awarded academic honors."
– "He was honorably discharged from the service."

But it sounds a bit dated in the 21st century to speak of someone as an "honorable man," or to lament a family's loss of honor.

What Is Honor?

To *honor* is "to show respect." It is an attitude and an act of recognition. It means acknowledging the worth or value of a person, institution, or object.

Honor can involve such things as:

- Dressing more formally in order to show respect for certain occasions or for the persons such occasions are set up to honor
- Gestures, such as opening doors, or pulling out chairs for women, standing up when introduced to guests, offering an elderly or infirm person one's seat—all intended to highlight the respect and care due to others in particular circumstances
- Addressing people with honorifics, such as "Father" (priests), "professor" (teachers and mentors), "Mr." or "Mrs." (new acquaintances, or children to adults), and so on—titles that show respect for the office they hold or the role they play in our lives, or which do not presume a familiarity we have not earned
- Defending someone's reputation from unjust attack or challenge.
- Refraining from the use of epithets and slang that deride or make fun of

holy things, persons, or institutions that should command our respect
- ■ Providing financially for parents, spending personal time with aging relatives to make sure that their lives are going well, and that they have what they need

Which is to say that honor, far from being obsolete, is a basic element in human life. Whatever terms we use—honor, recognition, esteem—the reality is that every culture finds ways to express the values it attaches to people, behavior, and institutions. The problem for us in the 21st century is that past cultures tended to honor social relationships and responsibilities, social order and office—*persons*, in other words – while contemporary attitudes tend to value function and performance. This is an important thing to notice.

Honor in our society accrues to sports figures and celebrities, scientists and astronauts, artists, along with the occasional humanitarian—people who are seen to have accomplished something noteworthy, or who perform in some extraordinary way. But even this honor extended by our society tends to be provisional. The pervasive notion of equality as sameness—"I'm just as good as the next guy"—means that our distinguished figures, paradoxically, must validate their uniqueness by vigorously asserting that they're just like everyone else. One sees this routine on particularly vivid display at Academy Awards ceremonies and the Kennedy Center honors.

This "subverted esteem" syndrome so characteristic of our age, in which society needs to honor people, but insists that they decline it, is also aided and abetted by the dominant casual style of consumerist life. Increasingly, we live in a leisure-oriented society in which there is a positive distaste for culturally mandated manifestations of respect, for dressing up, for formal ceremony, for any circumstance in which we can't behave according to the dictates of the moment.

I am reminded of the current cultural battle over one of the last bastions of formal culture in our society: the concert hall. Cultural critics for some time now have been waging what can only be called a battle against the wearing of formal attire by either audiences or performers at classical music concerts. Whereas the battle has largely been lost in the case of audiences, symphony musicians, for the most part, still wear tuxedos and black dresses when playing Beethoven. The reason for the custom is clear enough: the formal clothing announces that the music we're hearing, and, indeed, the event we're attending has a sacramental feel—this is art on the highest plane. The culture of the concert separates (consecrates) its content from other perfectly legitimate but ordinary fare. In contrast to casual attire, formal dress shows respect for something higher, something not ordinary, something worthy of special honor.

This notion of higher and lower, of course, is itself at the core of any discussion of honor. Honor presupposes that some offices, occasions, achievements, and responsibilities are higher than others—that is, they have a greater objective worth, and, therefore, a greater claim on our respect—all notions that are under challenge in today's culture of mass individualism.

This purely functional sense of honor—in which relationships are largely formless and subject to the whims of fashion—has powerfully negative effects on many vital aspects of everyday life:

- It subverts the educative role of the family and the role of parents as first teachers of their children. With so many competing (and equivalent) sources of authority, children no longer know how to evaluate (and honor) what their parents say.
- It weakens the effectiveness of all authority structures by reducing the respect due certain offices to likeability or some aspect of performance.
- It undermines the respect and assent of mind that Christians owe the truths of the Gospel by giving the greatest weight to personal opinion and the spirit of the times.
- It marginalizes the elderly whose wisdom and experience have no place in a worldview based on youth and physical prowess.

This, of course, is not to say that everything about traditional culture, or the way things worked in the past, was wonderful, or that everything about modern egalitarian culture is bad. For example, no one wants to revive a culture of honor that makes people stiff and formal with each other or which freezes people into rigid social classes. Modern culture mandates a relaxed, warm, affectionate relational environment—and that, too, is part of the Christian ideal.

Nevertheless, having a good and healthy culture of honor is vital for the proper functioning of human life and central to life in the Body of Christ. If our society provides a weak or ineffective model of honor, then we'll have no choice but to restore elements of honor that are missing from the equation. Charles Simpson, a noted charismatic teacher, aptly called honor "the atmosphere or attitude of community." **Honor is the attitude, the behavior that makes relationships work.**

Honor in the Bible

In Scripture, honor is a very important concept, indeed. In order to consider it in practical terms, we'll first have to grasp a vision of how great and encompassing a reality honor really is.

As is often the case, biblical Hebrew and Greek terms for honor do not have single, simple English equivalents. Several different Hebrew and Greek words are sometimes translated as *honor*. The principal Hebrew term is *kabod*. This word has the sense of weight or heaviness. It is sometimes translated *glory*—the *glory* of God is the weight or value attached to Him, in this case, an incalculable value. To give glory to God, as the Psalms constantly urge, is to render to God the supreme honor or weight (value) He commands.

The main New Testament Greek term is *time* (tee-meh). This Greek word carries with it the sense of price or preciousness. Both terms clearly refer to the value or worth of someone or something.

Honor, therefore, accrues to someone or something valuable. To render honor is to express our recognition of that value or worth. By contrast, to dishonor means either to fail to recognize someone's worth, or to commit an act that lessens or destroys the value that, by right, attaches to them.

While honor proceeds from an attitude—from an inner conviction about a person or thing, it is, by nature, manifested respect or esteem. Honor is not only something you *think*, but also something you *do*. The two—attitude and act—must go together. For example, to honor someone without really believing in his or her worth is called *flattery*. By definition, then, *honor* is "something conferred or given."

In Mark chapter 10, John and James, the sons of Zebedee, approach Jesus and ask for positions of power in the coming messianic kingdom. Jesus, after wondering whether they're really prepared to pay the price for power in the kingdom—namely, martyrdom, turns aside their request with this explanation:

> *"To sit at my right hand or at my left is not mine to grant, but it is for those for whom it has been prepared."* (Mark 10:35-40)

In other words, followers of Jesus are not to seek honors—even in the kingdom. (There are more than a few traces of comedy in this story of pride and youthful enthusiasm.) Honors are conferred on those for whom they're intended; they are granted, not sought.

We cannot help noticing that this marks a distinct difference between Christian culture—the culture of Christian love—and the culture of worldly esteem. In secular culture, honor or esteem is something one actively seeks. Performers spend years training and coming up through the ranks precisely in order to win the respect of peers and the public. Christians, on the other hand, are to give, to confer honor generously—but not to seek it for themselves or to organize their lives in order to attract it.

It is enough for a Christian clergyman to be a good priest; he is on dangerous ground if he sets out to be a famous one. Jesus Himself, the Letter to the Philippians movingly tells us, laid aside the honors that were His by right in order to redeem us.

Have this mind among yourselves, which is yours in Christ Jesus, who, though he was in the form of God, did not count equality with God a thing to be grasped, but emptied himself, taking the form of a servant, being born in the likeness of men. And being found in human form, he humbled himself and became obedient unto death, even death on a cross. Therefore, God has highly exalted him and bestowed on him the name which is above every name. (Philippians 2:5-9)

It's worth noting that while Jesus is prepared to "empty himself" of the honor due Him in order to fulfill His mission, God the Father "exalts" or honors Him for His sacrifice.

Showing and expressing honor is an essential part of the culture of the Christian people. Paul exhorts us:

Let love be genuine; hate what is evil, hold fast to what is good; love one another with brotherly affection; outdo one another in showing honor. (Romans 12:9-10)

Two things are worth noting here:

1. Paul connects honor with love. Honor is not only an expression of respect, but is part of what it means to love and cherish others.
2. Paul proposes that if there's to be competition among Christians, let us compete then in the arena of love—"outdo one another in showing honor," in manifesting the esteem in which we hold one another and the value we place on each other's lives and service.

Honor and God

The most important thing about honor is that it comes from God. It is an expression of the life of God Himself, and of the way God behaves. Jesus gives us a glimpse into the inner life of God in His public remarks after the healing of the paralytic at the Sheep Pool.

Jesus said to them, "Truly, truly, I say to you, the Son can do nothing of his own accord, but only what he sees the Father doing; for whatever he does, that the Son does likewise. For the Father loves the Son, and shows him all that he himself is doing; and greater works than these will he show him, that you may marvel....The Father judges no one, but has given all judgment to the Son, that all may honor the Son, even as they honor the Father. He who does not honor the Son does not honor the Father who sent him." (John 5:19-23)*

As the Prologue to John's Gospel indicates (John 1:1-14), the Father honored the Son in the beginning, before the world was created. In the passage above, we see God the Father honoring the Son by placing the Son as the unique gateway to Him.

In the Last Supper discourses in John, Jesus exalts the Holy Spirit whom the Father will send in His name:

"And I will pray to the Father and he will give you another Counselor, to be with you forever, even the Spirit of truth, whom the world cannot receive, because it neither sees him nor knows him....But the Counselor, the Holy Spirit, whom the Father will send in my name, he will teach you all things, and bring to your remembrance all that I have said to you." (John 14:16-17; 26)

These are supremely mysterious and complex Gospel passages, but, for our purposes, it's enough to point out that it is the nature of God to honor. He is honorable, and therefore, He honors. Honor is something rooted in the very character of God.

Honor in the Life of God's People

One of the most important passages on honor in Scripture is one of the most familiar: the Ten Commandments in Exodus 20:

And God spoke all these words, saying,

"I am the Lord your God, who brought you out of the land of Egypt, out of the house of bondage. You shall have no other gods before me.

You shall not make for yourself a graven image, or any likeness of anything that is in heaven above, or that is in the earth beneath, or that is in the water under the earth; you shall not bow down to them or serve them; for I am the Lord your God....

You shall not take the name of the Lord your God in vain; for the Lord will not hold him guiltless who takes his name in vain.

Remember the Sabbath day, to keep it holy. Six days you shall labor and do all your work, but the seventh day is a Sabbath to the Lord you God; in it you shall not do any work....

Honor your father and your mother, that your days may be long in the land which the Lord your God gives you.

You shall not kill.

You shall not commit adultery.

You shall not steal.

You shall not bear false witness against your neighbor. You shall not covet your neighbor's house; you shall not covet your neighbor's wife, or his man-servant, or his maidservant, or his ox, or his ass, or anything that is your neighbor's."

(Exodus 20:1-17)

These commandments, which outline fundamental biblical teaching about the way to live, revolve around the theme of honor:

1. I am the Lord: *Honor the Lord alone as God.* You can't honor, value, or treat anyone or anything—actually or in effect—as if he or it were God. The Lord alone is God. To dishonor God—to fail to recognize His role as Creator—has very real social consequences (see Romans 1:18-32, or consult your local newspaper).
2. *Honor the Lord's name.* Treat His name with reverence (with fear). Honoring the Lord's name has two basic applications:

    i.   We're not to use His name to commit perjury or to bear false witness against our neighbor (to dishonor God's name by using it as a means to cloak fraud or deception).
    ii. Honoring the Lord's name also means avoiding irreverent or insincere

uses of it (as an epithet, for example). Our speech should be filled with the praise of God, not cynical, ignorant, or joking references to holy persons and things.

3. *Honor the Sabbath Day.* We will discuss this topic in a later chapter. Suffice it to say here that keeping the Sabbath holy is a matter of honoring the saving deeds of God and imitating His rest—an anticipation of the life of heaven.
4. *Honor your father and your mother.* We are going to focus on this commandment. You might also take note of the comments made on this subject in the previous chapter.

St. Paul, writing a gloss on this commandment, says in Ephesians:

Children, obey your parents in the Lord, for this is right. "Honor your father and mother" (this is the first commandment with a promise), "*that it may be well with you and that you may live long on the earth." (Ephesians 6:1-3)**

The apostle is reflecting here on the wording of the fourth commandment in Deuteronomy 5:16:

Honor your father and your mother, as the Lord your God commanded you; that your days may be prolonged, and that it may go well with you, *in the land which the Lord your God gives you.* (Deuteronomy 5:16)*

We said in the previous chapter that honoring parents comes directly after the honor due to God in the Ten Commandments. As we noted there, this is not an accident. Its placement says, in effect, that you cannot say that you are honoring God, your Father in heaven, while dishonoring your parents, your father and mother on earth.

In Romans 1, in fact, the apostle lists being "disobedient to parents" as among the forms of wickedness that characterize godless societies (Romans 1:28-31). Not surprisingly, then, honoring parents is the first of the social commands—and the model for our relations with others. As the *Catechism* observes:

The fourth commandment opens the second table of the Decalogue. It shows us the order of charity. God has willed that, after him, we should

77

honor our parents to whom we owe life and who have handed on to us the knowledge of God. (*Catechism of the Catholic Church:* 2197)

As the Catechism also rightly points out, the honor due to parents is not absolute (2232). It is conditioned by our first obligation to honor God Himself and the call to become a disciple of Jesus (Matthew 10:37)—a vocation that the Christian family is instituted to foster.

The longer version of the commandment, however, in Deuteronomy and in Paul's citation of it, points us in the direction of a very important element in the honoring of parents: "that your days may be long"—the promise Paul notes in connection with the commandment.

Paul's comment on honoring parents comes in the middle of a long section in Ephesians on family life. (Ephesians 5:21-6:9) The apostle is saying two basic things:

i.   All Christian family life is grounded in this commandment. Hence, the welfare of the family is dependent on how parents are honored—both for the sake of the authority of the family and its integrity as an environment for education and training—and as a model for how the family conducts its affairs.

ii. Honoring parents is the principal means of ensuring the longevity and happiness of parents and as the means of establishing a kind of societal peace throughout the generations—of assuring the continued existence and prosperity of the family itself.

We noted in the previous chapter that honoring parents involves both respect and service—both an attentiveness to their authority and experience and a commitment to provide, in both personal and financial terms, for the needs of parents in old age. The biblical notion here is this: As your children witness the care you provide for your parents in infirmity and old age, they, too, following your good example, will care for you when you are old and vulnerable—thus ensuring peace between the generations and, provided the commandment is honored, the promise of security and welfare for future ones.

If, as we noted in the previous chapter, that there's a logic of gratitude, there's also a logic of honor: *honor begets honor*. Honor your parents and you stand a good chance of your children honoring you. Ideally, then, the very real benefits of honor—which ensure a good life, proper care, and a full legacy—will be passed on down the generations and produce the long life and prosperity of which the commandment speaks. It is not too much to say that honoring parents is the biblical key to successful living.

Again, as we have noted before, honor in the biblical sense nearly always implies two things: respect and money, or provision. When Paul, for example, urges that "elders who rule well be considered worthy of double honor, especially those who labor in preaching and teaching" (I Timothy 5:17), he's not encouraging a cascade of compliments but an increase in salary. Likewise, when the apostle exhorts that real widows be honored, he's talking about more than esteem—he's indicating that the Church should make proper financial provision for them on account of their service. (I Timothy 5:3)

Concerned, in fact, that some would-be servants of the Church are using their apostolic duties (or spiritual call) as an excuse to evade their familial responsibilities, Paul commands in the sternest possible language:

If anyone does not provide for his relatives, and especially for his own family, he has disowned the faith and is worse than an unbeliever. (I Timothy 5:8)

This same paradigm, or model, established in the commandment to honor parents is the key to understanding the rest of the social commandments. Honor, in every case, is the operative concept—honoring   life (which, since you did not give it, is not yours to take); honoring the reputation, possessions, spouses (life commitments) of others (which, in that they belong to someone else, are not yours to appropriate, misrepresent, or alienate).

Honor and Relationships
Using the model of honor to parents, let's look at some key relationships in our lives.

God: Father, Son, and Holy Spirit
We honor God by: worshipping Him and by tithing (providing resources).

Worshipping God

The Christian culture of honor we've been delineating in this chapter begins here, in our attempts to honor and glorify the Lord. For Catholics, the Mass provides the prototype: the special gestures of honor that surround the Scripture readings, the Gospel book, genuflections and bowing before the altar, the rituals that emphasize the central importance of the Eucharist Prayer, the Consecration and the sacred species.

What's important is that the honor expressed in worship is not merely interior. It involves outward expressions, gestures, and rituals. At the same time, it's not simply a matter of gestures, but of expressions that flow from attitudes of faith and love. Honor, by definition, involves both.

A good example of the essential unity of gesture and attitude has to do with a very contemporary issue: standards of dress at Mass. I think it's safe to say that most people who are indifferent about the way they dress for Mass—who feel free to wear the sort of casual clothing they'd wear at a barbecue or gym— have no intention of behaving disrespectfully toward the Lord or toward fellow parishioners. But what they've failed to grasp is that their casual clothing choices, in this context, convey meaning—they express something. While their hearts may be full of religious devotion (attitude), their clothing (gesture) indicates that there is nothing special about being in church—that it's a place like every other place, no different, in essence, from the barbershop or the filling station. There's a disconnect, doubtless born of a desire to be comfortable, that threatens to subvert the honor they intend to render to the Lord.

Dressing respectfully at Mass, or wearing your "Sunday best," as it used to be called, is an aspect of Catholic life and the culture of honor that urgently needs to be restored. A small gesture in itself, dressing in a special way for Mass or for other major religious observances indicates that this is no ordinary or casual event, but something set apart (holy), commanding the greatest respect and honor.

This point must be qualified by the respect due to the poor who may not be able to afford fine clothes for religious services (see James 2:1-6). The clothing issue I'm referring to has to do with fellow parishioners who are making a cultural rather than an economic statement.

Tithing

We honor God by tithing (providing resources). It's always a little surprising how much attention Scripture places on money and resources. But in both the Old and New Testaments, money is regarded as a very spiritual thing—not merely as a vehicle for paying clergy salaries and advancing mission, but, more fundamentally, as an icon or symbol of the person . As a Pentecostal minister friend once pointedly said, "Your money is *you*"—it represents you. Your spending habits, in fact, speak volumes about your real values and what you really honor in your life.

As we saw in the issue of honoring parents, money and resources play a large role in what it means to honor them. In the same way, allocating one's resources to God and to the work of His Church is not only a form of honoring God, but of worship.

Every Person

We are to honor all people, including the needy, because all men and women are made in the image and likeness of God, and crowned with His glory and honor.

Live as free men, yet without using your freedom as a pretext for evil, but live as servants of God. Honor all men. Love the brotherhood. Fear God. Honor the emperor. (I Peter 2:16-17)

He who oppresses a poor man insults his Maker, but he who is kind to the needy honors him. (Proverbs 14:31)

When I look at the heavens, the work of thy fingers, the moon and the stars which thou hast established, what is man that thou art mindful of him, and the son of man that thou dost care for him? Yet you have made him little less than God, and crowned him with glory and honor. (Psalm 8:3-5)

The source of human greatness is God Himself, and when we honor the image and likeness of God in others, regardless of their relationship to us or to the Gospel, we pay honor not only to them, but to the Source of that greatness. That's particularly the case when that divine image is obscured by need or disability. The saints show us the power of this fundamental Christian witness to the dignity of the person—for example, St. Francis of Assisi kissing the leper or Mother Teresa of Calcutta in our day who celebrated the humanity of the impoverished and dying.

Again, one notices here that St. Francis was not content merely to inwardly honor God's image in the leper, but he expressed it in a concrete (and courageous) gesture, and Mother Teresa did not simply respect the dignity of the abandoned of Calcutta in her heart, but created physical conditions in which they could die in peace and comfort.

Public Officials and Civil Institutions

Part of honoring all men and women also involves honoring those in secular authority—those in law enforcement and government.

Let every person be subject to the governing authorities. For there is no authority except from God, and those that exist have been instituted by God....Pay all of them their dues, taxes to whom taxes are due, revenue to whom revenue is due, respect to whom respect is due, honor to whom honor is due. (Romans 13:1, 7)

Needless to say, *respect* in this sense means addressing public officials by their proper titles, whether or not we agree with their policies or political philosophy. (Recall that when the Apostle Paul wrote the above lines about honoring governmental authority, Nero, one of history's most notorious persecutors of Christians, was emperor of Rome.) And, of course, as we saw in terms of parents, honor also means money—in this case, paying taxes and fulfilling other public fiscal obligations.

God's Servants

God's servants deserve honor. The pope, bishops, priests, deacons, consecrated religious—each in their own way—deserve honor and respect because of the offices they hold and because they represent God Himself and the order He has established in His Church. Lay leaders and mature Christians of proven wisdom and spiritual judgment also deserve respect because of the gifts God has given them. God Himself blesses the honor given to His servants.

As Jesus tells His disciples:

"He who receives you receives me, and he who receives me receives him who sent me. He who receives a prophet because he is a prophet shall receive a prophet's reward, and he who receives a righteous man because he is a righteous man shall receive a righteous man's reward."
(Matthew 10:40, 41)

As this passage indicates, the honor given to God's servants is really about honoring God, the source of their responsibilities and gifts—not, at least in a fundamental sense, about the particular personality who occupies the office.

Again, our culture can present particular challenges in this area. An acquaintance told me once of an incident in an Eastern Catholic parish where a biritual priest, who occasionally concelebrated there, felt uncomfortable with the traditional custom of lay people kissing the priest's hand when receiving a blessing. (The custom is a form of respect for the incalculable gifts that come to us through the hands of priests.) He was also ill at ease with other forms of respect directed toward him as a clergyman—a member of the "just call me Bob" school.

When an old babushka, a Russian grandmother, tried to kiss his hand at the end of Mass, he indignantly pulled his hand away to forestall the gesture. She promptly pulled his hand to her lips and kissed it.

"What!" she cried in exasperation. "You think this has something to do with *you*?"

She was telling him in a way I presume he never forgot that she demanded her right to respect the office and gift of the priesthood. It wasn't meant as a reward for his personal charms.

By the way, I don't advocate taking the babushka's emphatic, if not militant approach to expressing respect.

Family Members

We honor the members of the family.

Husbands and wives need to find ways to show respect for one another. Fundamentally, that is what the often-misunderstood New Testament passages on submission in marriage are all about (I Peter 3:1-7; Colossians 3:18, 19, and others.)

Husbands and wives need to build into their lives and the life of the family ways to acknowledge one another's particular contributions as husband and as wife. Doing this often involves overcoming a kind of culturally inspired embarrassment in expressing open and direct affection and appreciation. American culture normally favors the use of negative humor ("my old man," "the old ball-and-chain") or other indirect ways of expressing affection—expressing it by not expressing it. We need to learn to be open about our love and respect for one another and make such open and straightforward affection an operative part of everyday life—especially in the family.

This, as we indicated in the Gratitude chapter, will take creativity—not rules; it will take thought, prayer, and imagination.

In Proverbs 31, the famous passage on the virtuous wife, we have a good description of honor in the family:

Her children rise up and call her blessed; her husband, too, and he praises her:

"Many women have done excellently, but you surpass them all."

Charm is deceitful and beauty is vain, but a woman who fears the Lord is to be praised. Give her of the fruit of her hands, and let her works praise her in the [city] gates. (Proverbs 31:28-31)

Here, children praise their mother; the husband praises his wife, and not only in the bosom of the family, but at the city gates, where public life was conducted in the ancient world. Her fine and capable efforts to provide for her family do not merely earn her praise, however. Mirroring what we have seen in other scriptural passages on honor, she is given "the fruit of her hands"—in other words, material rewards for her work and greater responsibilities in response to her accomplishments.

Elderly Persons

We honor the elderly.

A hoary head is a crown of glory; it is gained in a righteous life. (Proverbs 16:31)

Do not rebuke an older man but exhort him as you would a father; treat younger men like brothers, older women like mothers, younger women like sisters, in all purity. Honor widows. (I Timothy 5:1-3a)

Two things should be noted here:

1. In contrast to trends in our own society, the biblical model envisions an *increase* in honor as one grows in age—the Book of Proverbs' refers to a "crown of glory [honor]." In the ancient world, retirement meant the possibility of assuming public office or finding leisure to harvest a lifetime of experience and wisdom in teaching and mentoring, or in a memoir or work of practical philosophy.

   Passing on one's experience to younger generations and creating a legacy remains a vital task for the elderly today—one, alas, too often left to the last minute when there's not sufficient time or energy. Part of honoring the old is not losing the benefit of their wisdom and perspective—including the testimony of their mistakes. As I often tell my own kids, "Make some new mistakes, will you?"

2. Like honoring parents, the increase in honor that attaches to old age also involves practical provision for their needs. One of the difficult—but necessary tasks of communities and parish groups is developing plans for the care of the aged. With the skyrocketing costs of elder care, and the isolated leisure world cocoons that are often created to warehouse the aged today, it behooves Christians to ensure that elderly brothers and sisters are properly supported and, finally, able to die in the midst of people who love them, in a Christian and dignified manner. This, as everyone concerned will attest, is no easy task. We, too, in our community are struggling to make a meaningful response to the social, familial, and financial challenges posed by aging and the needs of the dying.

The Dead

We honor the dead.

In a related sense, we must also defy the tenor of the times in isolating and sanitizing the experience of death and burial. Death is a part of life, and must be integrated back into Christian culture—both in a liturgical and in a domestic sense (the Christian wake, annual celebrations of the anniversaries of death, memorials, and other remembrances and honors).

The first and foremost aspect of this honor, of course, has to do with proper and reverent burial—one of the corporal works of mercy, as the *Catechism* points out.

> The bodies of the dead must be treated with respect and charity, in faith and hope of the Resurrection. The burial of the dead...honors the children of God, who are temples of the Holy Spirit. (*Catechism of the Catholic Church:* 2300)

But honor also involves developing ways of remembering the dead in families and communities—in making sure that they remain a part of us, that we see ourselves connected to that larger memory, the greater community of the Church, living and dead, and—much closer to home—in spiritually recalling the reality of death as a reminder to us, the living, that life is short and that choices matter.

Practical Comments on Expressing Honor

Let me conclude with some practical comments on expressing honor.

First, we do need to take seriously that honor is manifested esteem, that honor means actions in addition to attitudes. It's important, as we've said before, not to legislate a lot of arbitrary or artificial norms, lest we get ourselves all tangled up in rules and regulations and miss the good and up-building life that honor has for its aim. Different cultures will also have important contributions to make to the discussion of specifics—the rule here being: the more organic the custom the better; build from what you already know or do.

Having said that, however, specific behaviors do matter. I want to make one suggestion that seems, to me at least, to be where honor starts in a practical sense—a behavior so simple and so essential that it will challenge most of us for the rest of our lives.

The most basic sign of respect you can extend to a person is to acknowledge his or her existence. How often have I sat in a meeting, with people coming and going, and, focused on the business at hand, never once acknowledged they were even there? Or, how often have I been engrossed by what I was reading and, with head firmly buried in book, hoped that the people who'd come into the room wouldn't interrupt me?

Do you wish to grow in honor? Then, make a habit of acknowledging and recognizing other people. (In the end, isn't acknowledging another the essence of honor: the recognition of beings for what they really are?) You might rise when brothers and sisters come into a room and give them a warm greeting. If you're busy with a task, you might stop or take a break in what you're doing and greet the people approaching you. Such gestures say something very important. They say to the person greeted: You're more important than what I'm doing. You're more important than the task of the moment. I acknowledge you, I recognize your worth, and I value your presence in my life.

Nothing is more important than this.

Second, that honor, in the sense that we're talking about it, is about a great deal more than being polite. Courtesy and good manners are involved, but the honor the Lord wishes to restore as a part of building brotherhood and sisterhood, as a part of the culture of His people, is a large, encompassing reality; it is a whole approach to relationships. As Paul the Apostle stresses, honor is an important part of love, a way to reverence one another, a way to treat one another with the respect we are due as God's creatures, as beings God Himself honors, and as brothers and sisters of Christ. (Romans 12:9-10)

In practice, honor is supposed to help relationships come alive by enabling people to experience through the actions of others their own inestimable value. This is not in some generic, one-size-fits-all sort of way, but, precisely, as men; as women; as husbands and wives, fathers and mothers; as children; as priests and religious; as widows and single people; as the aged. Ideally, the culture of honor helps us all to live with each other more easily, to lay aside the natural defenses we all put up against love and one another, and to relax in each other's company—permitted, at last, by the esteem we find in each other, to do what we've always wanted to do—to give and receive love.

Speaking the truth in love, we are to grow up in every way into him who is the head, into Christ, from whom the whole body, joined and knit together by every joint with which it is supplied, when each part is working properly, makes bodily growth and up builds itself in love. (Ephesians 4:15-16)

Things to Think and Pray About

Honor is both an attitude of recognizing (truly seeing) and acknowledging beings for who and what they are and appropriate expressions of this recognition that undergird the social commandments and make relationships work. Honor is the key to social happiness and peace.

- "Honor is the social witness given to human dignity." (*Catechism of the Catholic Church:* 2479)
- "Honor is the atmosphere, the attitude of community." (Charles Simpson)
- "Love one another with brotherly affection; outdo one another in showing honor." (Romans 12:10)
- "Of courtesy—it is much less than courage of heart and holiness. Yet in my walk it seems to me that the grace of God is in courtesy." (Hilaire Belloc)

Chapter 6
Reliability and Kindness

But the fruit of the Spirit is love, joy, peace, patience, kindness, goodness, faithfulness, gentleness, self-control.

Galatians 5:22

For the grace of God has appeared for the salvation of all men, training us to renounce irreligion and worldly passions, and to live sober, upright, and godly lives in this world.

Titus 2:11-12

When thinking about Christian love, it's easy to focus on high ideals and biblical theology. Facing the practical, on-the-ground realities of our actual relationships—how we really behave toward one another, how we love one another in everyday circumstances—this is not so easy. And yet this is often where the rubber meets the road in living the Gospel as a way of life. Christianity is shockingly practical.

I've written that a number of these chapters come out of surprising experiences. This one is no exception. At first glance, it might seem odd (or redundant) that we identify reliability as one of the building blocks of spiritual culture. But, in practice, what I've found over the years is that (apparently) small or habitual failures of personal responsibility and what another age would have called "character"—the sort of things that happen over the backyard fence or at a parish yard sale or on chore day or at a wedding, in fact, anytime—can loom large. If not addressed they can have significant and lasting effects on the level of trust and respect people have (and can have) for one another.

In my experience, people really do want to trust each another. But in practice, we all have to work hard in order to enable our brothers and sisters to do just that. This chapter focuses on a number of very practical areas of Christian relationships and culture that can become sore points and obstacles in people's paths to love and trust if we do not have a common appreciation of, and approach to them. A Christian group, of whatever size or complexion, overlooks issues of reliability and character at its own peril.

Being Faithful to One's Word

Lord, who shall be admitted to your tent and dwell on your holy mountain?...He who keeps his pledge, come what may...Such a man will stand firm forever. (Psalm 14:1, 4a, 5b)*

Many a man proclaims his own loyalty, but a faithful man who can find? A righteous man who walks in his integrity—blessed are his sons after him! (Proverbs 20:6, 7)*

But above all, my brethren, do not swear, either by heaven or by earth, or with any other oath, but let your yes be yes and your no be no, that you may not fall under condemnation. (James 5:12)

The dictionary defines *integrity* as "whole, entire, of one piece, undivided"—in other words, what you see is what you get. To lack integrity is to be a divided person, to be of two minds, whose intentions are not (or not always) clear. One of the most important positive aspects of godly speech is cultivating the habit of fidelity to one's word—the simple, direct, unguarded, and trustworthy speech that the Scriptures praise. *Let your yes be yes and your no, no.* (Matthew 5:37)

The simple rule here is: If you *say* you're going to do something, *do it.* Your integrity and credibility rises or falls on whether you do or do not keep your word. This not only involves keeping specific promises and commitments, but also other instances in which you've simply said you would do something.

If you habitually fail to keep your word in so-called little things, people do take note—perhaps quiet, unspoken note—but notice nonetheless, and it affects their ability to trust you or your intentions. It doesn't mean people don't love you or care about you, but it may mean that they have discovered that they can't trust you.

Clearly, one of the things that has to change in order to acquire the habit of being faithful to one's word is the carelessness with which we commonly speak to one another. Don't be too quick to assure someone that you'll do something if, in fact, you're uncertain about your ability to perform or complete the task. This, of course, is an inner, mental discipline that takes seriously the needs and requests of others and soberly and realistically assesses whether or not we have the resources or the time to genuinely fulfill them. Otherwise, what we unconsciously communicate to other people is that we will do what we told them we would do—if and when it's convenient for us.

If one has a problem being realistic about time or commitments—many of us do—enlist the aid and counsel of someone who is good at it—who has good judgment about time.

It's always better to ask someone for time to think about a request than to promise the moon and fail to deliver. In Christian terms, this is called *sobriety*—"to be a sober, awake, attentive person." One who is "quick to hear, slow to speak" (James 1:19), who no longer lives in a dream world, but who takes people and commitments seriously.

Often, in our society, promises are quickly and glibly made in order to appease people, to get them off our backs, or to keep them from being disappointed—only to cause them even greater discomfort when we fail to keep our word or remember what we've agreed to do.

These small problems are like little abrasions—individually not significant—but when added up, or when a matter of habit or routine, become, over time, real injuries, with real consequences.

Obviously, if there's a problem, or we've been optimistic about the amount of time fulfilling a request will take, we can go to the person to whom we've made the promise and ask to move the deadline to a more reasonable date.

- "I know I said I would do this for you by the 12th, but it just doesn't look feasible. May I get it to you by the 20th instead?"

Usually people will be understanding, and respect you for letting them know about the delay in advance. Just don't take advantage of this escape clause too often.

Loaning and Borrowing Property

"In his use of things man should regard the external goods he legitimately owns not merely as exclusive to himself but common to others also, in the sense that they can benefit others as well as himself." *The ownership of any property makes its holder a steward of Providence*, with the task of making it fruitful and communicating its benefits to others, first of all his family. (*Catechism of the Catholic Church:* 2404)*

In our consumerist culture, things are "stuff"—disposable commodities that are used and used up at will, and largely for people's personal convenience or recreation. By contrast, possessions and property, in the biblical sense, are trusts. We are given possessions on loan, as it were, from the Provident God, to manage as stewards, for our own good and for the good of others.

The Lord places goods at our disposal to allow us to care for ourselves, our families, and others: to build the kingdom of God. Because we are stewards of these good gifts, we are called to care for them and to see to it that they are used properly. Part of that proper use is a willingness to be generous with our possessions and to make them available to others.

Goods of production—material or immaterial—such as land, factories, practical or artistic skills, oblige their possessors to employ them in ways that will benefit the greatest number. Those who hold goods for use and consumption should use them with moderation, reserving the better part for guests, for the sick and the poor. (*Catechism of the Catholic Church:* 2405)

That's the basic principle, and it's an important one in view of the very different approach to possessions taken by our society—in which brand names, real estate, and car models are used as indices of personal status and worth—rather than as gifts held in trust for the kingdom.

Lending

Having said that, we should note some common problems that emerge in groups of fervent, prayerful, openhearted Christians about the use (and abuse) of goods. The points sketched out below, I assure you, reflect some unhappy experiences in this area. These eventually cause us to appreciate the importance of another key virtue in building healthy Christian relationships: that of prudence.

The virtue of prudence, one of the traditional four cardinal virtues — temperance, fortitude, justice, and prudence — is defined in the Catechism as:
The virtue that disposes practical reason to discern our true good in every circumstance and to choose the right means of achieving it; "the prudent man looks where he is going." (Proverbs 14:15) Prudence is "right reason in action," writes St. Thomas Aquinas. (*Catechism of the Catholic Church:* 1806)

In First Peter, the apostle urges Christians to "keep sane and sober for your prayers." (I Peter 4:7) Prudence is the gift of sanity. In the interests of such sanity, let me recommend the following points for your consideration:

First of all, while we are stewards of our possessions, that doesn't imply that everything we own belongs by right to the community or the parish. What belongs to you is yours—you, after all, are its steward. Hence, you have the right to refuse to lend something or, if you do, to dictate the terms under which you will lend it.

For example, an item may have a high value for you, but be of less apparent value to another person: tools of your trade, heirloom china, a lace tablecloth made by your grandmother, first-edition books, and golf clubs.

You have every right to refuse to lend such precious items or to specify certain care requirements if you do. It's only prudent for the lender to ask the borrower how he or she intends to use the item you're loaning. For example:

- You'll want to know if someone plans to use your domestic sewing machine to mend a heavy canvas awning or use your valuable Waterford crystal bowl as a temporary planter.
- You'll want to know if your neighbor plans to use your finishing sander to smooth a concrete patch on his driveway or employ your best wood chisel as a screwdriver.
- You'll want to know if someone plans to use your lawn mower to attack a field of six-foot-high weeds behind his house.
- You'll want to know if your grandmother's lace tablecloth is going to be used as a background on which photographs are to be stapled.
  If you're loaning an item, particularly one of value, it's only prudent to inquire:
  - If the borrower knows how to use and clean it—for the sake of the item, surely, but also, and more importantly, for the borrower's sake and for the sake of your relationship.
  - If the borrower can specify the length of time he'll need the item or when he plans to return it.

Other prudent steps in lending might include putting your name on loaned items, or, if you have loaned out a great many items, keeping a written record of loan arrangements. Again, this is done not out of fussiness, but out of a certain realism about human relationships—prudence, again—and out of a desire to keep relationships clean, free from misunderstandings that a little care can avoid, and to prevent little things from getting in the way of the greater work of love.

A final realistic observation: *expect accidents to happen*—even when every care has been taken to avoid them. When they do, the lender must be prepared to deal with the borrower charitably; ease his or her concerns; note any lessons the situation may contain for the future, and move on.

Borrowing
The wicked man borrows without repaying, but the just man is generous, and gives. (Psalm 36:21)

The origins of the word *borrow* imply more than the simple promise to return a borrowed item to its owner. Borrowing also entails a pledge to care for the object borrowed, to take heed, to ensure that it is safe in our hands. It is part of the moral character of the transaction: In response to the generosity of the lender (Psalm 36:21), the borrower not only makes use of, but pledges to protect—in other words, to steward—the property he has received.

　–"Thanks so much, Charlie, for the use of your power-saw; I'll take good care of it, just as you would."

If you're not prepared to make that commitment, or if the item requested requires, on reflection, more care and maintenance than you're capable of providing, then don't borrow it.

In effect, the Christian relational equation is this: let the one be generous and let the other be responsible. In this way, a habit of generosity in our relationships gets fostered and established in our lives.

Borrowing Responsibly

▸ **Return borrowed items in as good or better condition than when you received them.**

Before borrowing the item, it's always prudent to note its condition and ask the owner about flaws and quirks. Make sure you know how to use the item you've borrowed, what kind of maintenance it requires, and whether special care must be taken in cleaning it.

For example, if you borrow a car, make sure the owner briefs you on any specific problems or quirks. Of course, you should replace the gas you use, but, as a courtesy, you might consider returning it full, or, as a gesture of appreciation, give it a wash.

▸ **Return a borrowed item to its owner immediately after use.**

A common problem is to borrow an item, stick it someplace, and then forget about it. (Also, don't assume that because the owner gave you permission to use an item that this means you're free to loan it to someone else without first getting the owner's permission.)

For example, let's say someone borrows another's brand new barbecue grill. Six months later, the owner discovers it, unwashed, on the borrower's deck, where it's been sitting out in the rain for six months.

Or, for example, let's say that someone borrows a volume from another's valuable reference set, and then loses track of it. When the owner asks, after a few months, if he's finished with it, the borrower can no longer even remember whether he borrowed the book or not. The owner finds the valuable volume—which he has had to replace in the meantime—some years later in the 10 cents box at a parish rummage sale.

▷ **Restitution for borrowed items broken or damaged while in your possession is your (the borrower's) responsibility.**

If a man borrows anything of his neighbor, and it is hurt or dies, the owner not being with it, he shall make full restitution. (Exodus 22:14)

As we noted earlier, the lender ought to factor accidents into his or her own calculations in lending items out and ought to be prepared to handle the situation charitably. But the borrower's responsibility is—at the very least—to offer to replace or restore the item. This is particularly the case when carelessness or negligence in the treatment of the item is involved. The owner, as we have noted, may indicate that restitution is not expected or required, but it is the duty of the borrower to take full responsibility for the damage and to offer to pay for the item.

Again, these are not so much rules and regulations as they are indicators of the kind of care and courtesy that ought to characterize Christian life. This is the way we ought to treat each other.

Paradoxically, accidents, mistakes, and failings in our relationships, when met and faced responsibly, with character, and sensitivity, can end up enhancing our commitment to one another.

Let me give an example: A person borrowed an expensive set of crystal wine glasses from a good friend for a party she was hosting, having no suitable glasses of her own. The glasses were not only costly in dollars and cents, but a treasured wedding gift. An accident occurred at the event and a large number of the glasses were broken. The borrower, of course, apologized profusely. On a limited budget, she could not hope to pay for, or replace the expensive set she had borrowed, and so the lender told her not to worry about it—concluding that it had been imprudent to lend out such fragile and precious items. Despite the resolution, a subtle chill descended on the friendship between the two women, on what had been before a close and trusting bond.

Eager to do something to ease the situation, the borrower decided that while she could not afford to replace the broken goblets all at once, she could afford to replace them one at a time. And so, each year, at birthdays and at

Christmas, the young couple received a single crystal goblet from their friend, replacing yet another of the valuable ones that had been broken. Their relationship was not only restored, but deepened and enriched by this act of consideration.

Free Services

While we're on the subject of money (or restitution), let me comment briefly on the problem with expecting free services.

In communities and parishes, we often draw upon each other's skills or on expertise people have acquired in their line of work. In my experience, people are eager to lend a hand to help or advise brothers and sisters in the Lord, or to lend their professional skills to parish projects. This is to be expected; it's part of the generosity of spirit the Lord inspires, part of serving others with the riches of our experience. However, we should not assume that such services, because they are rendered to fellow Christians, are *free*.

We ought not to assume that professional services—auto repairs, plumbing or electrical work or advice, legal or investment counsel, internet or web services will be done on a volunteer basis, or that we can pick another's brain at will without offering remuneration at some point. Doubtless, those who have professional skills will approach payment for their services in different ways. Some may choose to volunteer their help or refuse to accept payment from parishioners or for parish work, or to donate their work under certain circumstances, but not others.

Brothers and sisters in the Lord typically will be generous with their time and resources. Generosity of spirit is something that the Lord Himself produces in us. What we shouldn't do is **presume** on that generosity—or take advantage of it. That's unjust.

What causes problems in relationships is when there are different expectations in this regard, or where arrangements are not adequately spelled out. **Never, ever rely on unspoken, unacknowledged assumptions. Make explicit agreements and don't skimp on the details. Believe it or not, it's part of the work of love.**

Being on Time

Time is one of our most precious resources, and one of the greatest gifts we are called upon to steward. Being punctual shows respect to the people in our lives and also cultivates fidelity to one's word and commitments. Along with the other areas touched on in this chapter, carelessness about time can be a major barrier in building relationships of trust and love.

Everyone experiences occasional difficulties in this area. Something comes up— an unexpected phone call, soccer practice is extended, unusual traffic conditions. If we discover that we're going to be late, it's important to make a serious effort to inform those waiting. This is common courtesy. From my perspective, however, social standards in this area appear to be loosening. These days many people are late, some habitually.

For some, the problem seems to be packing schedules too fully, trying to do too much. This, of course, is in itself a problem worth pondering: Why am I packing my schedule so tightly? Is it that I can't say no to people? Do I avoid being direct with people by agreeing to everything and anything, regardless of the demands already placed on my time? Is it that I haven't sorted out and placed priorities on my commitments?

For others, it seems that they're simply not that aware of time. They lose themselves easily in the luxury of the moment, and lose track of the rest of the day and the others who have claims on their time and attention.

Cultural differences, of course, can play a role here and should be factored into the standards we set, but culture can also be used as an excuse to avoid confronting an area of basic righteousness. The values of the Gospel are not only meant to be integrated with and within cultures, they are also meant to challenge aspects of culture.

If we find ourselves habitually late, we need first of all to face that our lack of punctuality is a serious problem, and that, whether we're aware of it or not, it affects our relationships with brothers and sisters in Christ. We ought to examine soberly why we're late. Does the fact that we're routinely late for certain appointments and activities reveal hidden attitudes we entertain toward people in our lives or reservations we have toward the commitments we've made?

In my experience, habitual lateness doesn't usually change decisively for the better until someone who's inconvenienced by it on a regular basis openly confronts the person, and refuses to accept his or her (usually creative) excuses. Change may also require practical help from someone who has good time management skills.

In any case, lateness that is the result of our own fault should require asking for forgiveness from whoever is affected. It's wrong. Even when our lateness is not a matter of our own fault, but due to unanticipated circumstances, an apology is in order.

It should be noted, however, that even with correction and counseling, some people will just be late. At some point, patience and forbearance may be the order of the day. Patience with others' shortcomings is a part of Christian life.

Kindness

For this very reason make every effort to supplement your faith with virtue, and virtue with knowledge, and knowledge with self-control, and self-control with steadfastness, and steadfastness with godliness, and godliness with brotherly affection [kindness], and brotherly affection [kindness] with love. (2 Peter 1:5-7)*

Put on then, as God's chosen ones, holy and beloved, compassion, kindness, *lowliness, meekness, and patience.* (Colossians 3:12)*

Many of the behaviors we've been considering in this chapter, in the end, have to do with the quality of graciousness, or kindness.

It's an expression of kindness as well as virtue to be faithful to one's word, or lend or borrow responsibly; it is kind as well as right not to leave someone waiting. I stress this quality of graciousness because the admonitions about fidelity and punctuality can sometimes come off as hard line or severe. While it's important that we take the admonitions seriously, it's even more important that we understand them in the context of love.

Even prudence—that virtue we cited in connection with lending and borrowing—is about wisely refraining from placing brothers and sisters in positions they may not be able to (or have proven that they cannot) handle. Choosing not to take risks in lending that might result in bad feelings or mistrust or, worse, wrongdoing—in the end, this, too, is about kindness, the care that we should take in our relationships, the sense of responsibility we have for one another.

In addition to being faithful, prudent, and punctual, we must also be gracious and considerate in our behavior toward one another.

When invitations include an RSVP, do we respond promptly, or ignore the legitimate concerns of the organizers, and show up anyway?

Do we habitually express gratitude to one another for services rendered, gifts given, or advice offered—or just take them for granted?

Do we cultivate gracious habits such as sending notes (through whichever medium), thanking people for doing favors, or lending us tools, or volunteering to babysit—or do we think about it, but never manage to do it?

Cultivating a parish and family culture marked by graciousness and kindness is more than good manners. It's a way to encourage us, in the midst of an increasingly solitary and self-centered culture, to be more person-oriented. More than this, an atmosphere of graciousness in our relationships encourages and spreads the effects of goodness.

Some final thoughts:

First of all, the perspectives on Christian behavior sketched out here, are, as we noted earlier, a matter of character. Being men and women of our word, being responsible stewards of our resources, time, and one another—the life of the virtues—is part of the good human culture that must undergird our efforts to build brotherhood and sisterhood in Christ. Just as the social realities of family and neighborhood, as we discussed in an earlier chapter, provide the basic underlying context for Christian community and for the parish, so basic personal character and discipline provide the foundation of Christian love.

Many years ago, in a charismatic community in Los Angeles , a priest once asked one of the leaders of a single men's household about the household's spiritual regimen.

"Well, we're teaching them to pray all right," replied the leader, "but the first order of business is getting them to *make their beds in the morning.*"

This is not always the easiest perspective for people to grasp—that making beds is spirituality's first order of business—but it is an essential perspective. Spirituality, for many, tends in the direction of high aspirations, exalted feelings and communion with the divine. And such experiences are part of the equation. But our efforts to love and serve God and one another do not (and cannot) rest on such a foundation. Loving God and neighbor—the essence of what it means to build brotherhood and sisterhood in Christ—is built not on the sand of inspiration, but on the solid rock of character.

If we don't pay attention to these practical aspects of Christian love and don't train our children in these basic virtues, we only pave the way for resentment, anger, and division to grow in our relationships and, eventually, to create a kind of toxic undercurrent in our efforts to respond to grace. In my experience, groups that fail to cultivate a culture of fidelity and responsibility do not, in the long term, survive.

In the end, reliability, responsibility, and graciousness are simply practical manifestations of the work of love.

Owe no one anything, except to love one another; for he who loves his neighbor has fulfilled the law. The commandments, "You shall not commit adultery, you shall not kill, you shall not steal, you shall not covet," and any other commandment, are summed up in this sentence, "You shall love your neighbor as yourself." Love does no wrong to a neighbor; therefore, love is the fulfilling of the law. (Romans 13:8–10)

Things to Think and Pray About

The trust between members of any Christian community is based on the consistent practice of kindness, graciousness, responsibility and faithfulness in even (apparently) small practical everyday matters.

- "Thoughtfulness is the beginning of great sanctity." (Mother Teresa of Calcutta)
- The Lord places goods at our disposal to allow us to care for ourselves, for our families, and for others, to build the kingdom of God.
- Prudence is the realism that seeks to prevent little things from getting in the way of love.
- "Kindness has converted more sinners than by zeal, eloquence, or learning." (Frederick William Faber)
- "Be kind for everyone is fighting a great battle." (Philo of Alexandria)
- "We must be more kind than just. Kindness alone conciliates." (St. John Chrysostom)

Chapter 7
Repairing Relationships

*One's capacity and ability to love, understand, and console an-
other is not dependent upon the degree to which one's love is
returned. If I could only love another human being to the degree
that they returned my love, I would probably have given up loving people a long time ago. Jesus also understood this kind of
love. He said, if someone borrows your shirt, do not expect it to
be returned (and he went further and said, "Give him your coat
as well."). This may sound like a one-way street—one person
continually trying to understand and love others and often receiving little or nothing in return. Ah, but the reward is not in receiving another's reciprocity—the reward is in the joy of loving
itself.*

S. Schimmel, from *Wounds Not Healed by Time:
The Power of Repentance & Forgiveness*

*Above all, let your love for one another be constant, for love co-
vers a multitude of sins.*

I Peter 4:8

Sometimes people have the impression that if you live in a Christian
community, if you're part of a vibrant Catholic parish, if you're a devout Catholic family, if you live in a convent or monastery where
everyone has dedicated his or her life to God, all will be well. Young
people, before marriage, often make similar rosy assumptions about family life:
I've found my soul mate; we've both got great and fulfilling careers; we've made
wise financial plans; we love each other—a sure path to a happy, untroubled
life.

Real communities, real parishes, and real families assume no such thing. In
fact, experience teaches that things will go awry each and every day; we will
hurt and disappoint one another each and every day—this, despite clear objec-
tives, talks, training, planning, dedication and all the good will in the world.

In the end, our best intentions are no match for original sin.

Repairing Relationships

Far from an occasional unpleasant necessity, the need for forgiveness and
the work of repairing relationships is a regular and critical part of Christian life.
The teaching of Jesus about forgiving your brother "seventy times seven" im-

plies as much. In real life, repentance and forgiveness aren't things you think about once a year or during Lent.

Unless Christian groups of whatever size and complexion have clear, simple procedures in place for dealing with wrongdoing, and, more importantly, for reconciliation, for repairing relationships, and this as a fundamental part of daily life, they'll quickly find themselves in serious, debilitating trouble—awash in quarrels, hurt, and alienation.

This is one of the reasons our own early experiments in trying to build community in Phoenix were so often fraught with difficulty and misunderstandings. Not only were there different views on how to approach community, but there were also hurt feelings, problematic personal histories, and the fallout from bad relational habits. In that we didn't really know how to handle such difficulties, they easily dominated the proceedings and made everyone miserable.

Fortunately, the early leaders of the covenant community movement, drawing on Scripture and the traditional wisdom of the Church, came up with some simple and effective principles about how to approach wrongdoing and repair damaged or broken relationships. These principles have proven themselves time and time again to be an indispensable tool in the work of Christian love. It's not too much to say that our community would not be here today if we had not been taught a way of life sustained by the wisdom and grace—and, yes, the *joy* of forgiveness.

One of the New Testament's most trenchant insights about forgiveness in the Christian life is found in Ephesians 4:

Be angry but do not sin; do not let the sun go down on your anger, *and give no opportunity to the devil.* (Ephesians 4:26)*

The underlying idea here is that while difficulties and wrongdoing will occur among Christians, they should be handled quickly, not allowed to fester—thus providing opportunities for the devil to sow mischief and discord in the body. This is an essential perspective. Many of the hurts or difficulties we experience in everyday life are small. At least, they are initially: real or perceived slights, failures in communication, undisciplined speech, misdirected anger or irritation, withdrawal or withholding of affection. We can all attest from personal experience that resentments deriving from such small incidents, if held onto and entertained invariably morph into judgments and bad attitudes, becoming, in the process, much larger and more intractable evils. In this way, our resentments function like infections. They may begin with minor cuts, but, untreated, they can fester into serious wounds. As Paul observes in the passage on love in Corinthians:

Love is not resentful; it is not self-seeking; it is not prone to anger; neither does it brood over injuries. (I Corinthians 13:5)

How many times has one observed in one's own life, with deep dismay, the seed of personal animosity in a misheard or misinterpreted remark or a slight that one has exaggerated into a full-blown expression of disrespect or disdain? When one adds gossip and slander to such a concoction, it's easy to see how the infection of small hurts can spread and harm the whole body.

I've seen small problems morph into something large many times in my life—to the detriment of people far beyond the circle of those directly involved. One such incident stands out in my mind. I had asked a dear brother to make my travel arrangements for a foreign trip. When asked if he had made the necessary reservations, he told a lie and indicated that he had done so, but, in fact, he had not yet booked the tickets. When he got around to it, the original arrangements were no longer available, and the trip was saddled with unnecessary chaos and inconvenience as a result of his negligence.

By the time the issue was addressed, several months later, this small incident had, in the meantime, sown guilt, defensiveness, mistrust, and resentment into what had been an exemplary working and fraternal relationship. It served as one of the starting points for a gradual weakening of our brotherhood, and ended up affecting many, many others. It took decades to heal.

St. Paul, ever the realist, urges that Christians keep their relationships clean, free of such toxins—cleansing, through forgiveness and reconciliation, each day's worth of hurt and disappointment. Ideally, in the apostle's vision, the close of each day should find the community, the family, the parish, the rectory at peace—having addressed, corrected, and forgiven the day's wrongs.

One community I'm familiar with actually incorporated this notion into their daily spiritual regimen. Before retiring, household members gathered for a brief night prayer, during which members were invited to silently forgive anyone who had offended or hurt them that day, and, if the matter were serious, to decide then and there, in their own minds, how they would proceed the next day to address the problem.

The basic attitude described here involves **eager repentance**. Far from regarding repentance as a form of humiliation, or something against which we have to defend ourselves, something to be resisted, the vision of relationships I'm proposing sees repentance—and, therefore, asking for and receiving forgiveness—as gifts God provides for His people, a resource through which evil can be undone and freedom restored. Given God's manifest desire to forgive and heal us, our attitude should be to take every opportunity to renounce wrongdoing and be reconciled to God and our brothers and sisters.

An unwillingness to repair wrongdoing in relationships, a refusal to grant forgiveness is much more than a matter of sour grapes or bad attitude. It is a failure of love, and the greatest single barrier to unity – whether in a marriage, a convent, a parish council or a community.

The Word *Wrongdoing*

The term *wrongdoing* is used here to denote specific human actions that disrupt or hinder right personal relationships—the kind of loving relationships that God wants to characterize our life together as brothers and sisters in the Lord. Catholics may be more accustomed to the use of the word *sin*—and *wrongdoing*, as I'm using it, is certainly sinful. But the term *sin* has broader theological connotations—the reality of original sin, for example—and its use in this context can be misunderstood, in my experience, or get us off track into discussions of whether this or that sin is venial or mortal. There's also the problem that in contemporary society, the word *sin* is used almost exclusively to refer to immoral sexual conduct.

Sin in its biblical sense, in both Hebrew and Greek, means "to miss the mark." It's a complex term, involving other deeper dimensions, but its central meaning is clear—to sin is to miss God's mark, to fall short of the standard of His plan.

As the *Catechism*, quoting Vatican II's *Gaudium et Spes*, makes clear in its discussion of the nature of sin:

> What Revelation makes known to us is confirmed by our own experience. For when man looks into his own heart he finds that he is drawn toward what is wrong and sunk in many evils which cannot come from his good creator. Often, refusing to acknowledge God as his source, man has also upset the relationship which should link him to his last end; and at the same time *he has broken the right order that should reign within himself as well as between himself and other men and all creatures.* (*Catechism of the Catholic Church:* 401)

Wrongdoing, then, as we're using the term here, is sin in the realm of relational acts and attitudes—actions which have their origins in the disorders of the human soul, the patterns of a sinful world, and the work of the devil—but for which we can, and, indeed, must take responsibility. To fail to do so, or to leave the effects of wrongdoing unresolved in our relationships is to invite serious and destructive consequences. And, they're the kinds of things we do every day: telling lies, losing our tempers and saying hurtful things, willfully ignoring people, making commitments and breaking them, behaving irresponsibly with someone else's goods.

It's worth underlining, again, that while asking for and giving forgiveness require decisions on our part, the grace of reconciliation comes from the Lord Himself. The reconciliation we administer to one another is the work of His healing and redeeming love. That grace is nourished and made effective in our lives through prayer and frequent recourse to the grace of the sacraments, particularly the Sacrament of Reconciliation.

Obstacles and Evasions

The first task in repairing relationships, as well as for all of these Building Blocks of Spiritual Culture, is to take wrongdoing and the need for forgiveness seriously. One of the main obstacles we face in this area involves relational attitudes and habits we inherit from the secular culture.

As a whole, our culture trains us to handle wrongdoing in relationships through some form of indirection or evasion. This is a major practical challenge to the whole area of repairing relationships.

The Try Harder Approach

- "I was pretty dismissive of Antonio's ideas at the meeting. But that's water under the bridge now. I'll try to be more supportive the next time the board meets."
- "Judy acts like it really hurt her when I forgot to show up for her birthday party. I must learn to be more careful about that kind of thing in the future."

What the try harder approach fails to understand is that, although one has the intention of doing better in the future, one's actions have done real and present damage to the relationship, leaving behind a deposit of mistrust and suspicion. Simply passing over the problem one has created with unspoken good intentions becomes, in effect, a way of evading responsibility. What is required is more than private remorse, but a commitment to attempt to right the wrongs one has done.

As stated in "The Sacrament of Penance and Reconciliation" in the *Catechism:*

> Many sins wrong our neighbor. *One must do what is possible in order to repair the harm (e.g.,* return stolen goods, restore the reputation of someone slandered, pay compensation for injuries). Simple justice requires as much. (*Catechism of the Catholic Church:* 1459)*

Denial

By far the most common way our culture trains us to handle personal wrongdoing comes in the form of denial—pretending or acting as if it didn't happen.
– "Well, listen, that's okay. I know you didn't really mean it!
– "Oh, forget it! I don't really mind that much."
– "Actually, I thought it was pretty funny, even if the joke was on me!"

The "Oh, that's okay" approach to dealing with personal wrongdoing is, of course, a way of *not* dealing with it—a form of evasion, an attempt to dismiss or minimize problematic incidents and attitudes, to laugh it off.

Three attitudes are at work in modern American culture's denial approach to wrongdoing: the myth of invulnerability, the primacy of emotions, and the lack of a simple procedure or mechanism.

THE MYTH OF INVULNERABILITY

This comes with the pioneer spirit and American can-do-ism—the ideal of being tough, of putting on a brave, self-confident and cheerful face in social situations, and, by contrast, avoiding anything that smacks of weakness, sensitivity, vulnerability or failure. "That's OK," in this sense, means that nobody can really hurt me.

THE PRIMACY OF EMOTIONS

As we've seen in discussions of other aspects of Christian culture, American mores privilege the emotions as unique arbiters of meaning and significance. "That's OK" here means that I'm not feeling particularly terrible about what you did, or ready to burst into tears over what you said. Given that, the incident of wrongdoing must not be all that important—it's better just to ignore it.

But the point isn't whether a particular act of wrongdoing makes us feel bad or not at any particular moment. Wrongdoing affects our relationships regardless of passing emotions—often in ways we don't realize right away, and that only show up later. In any case, our emotional temperature is not a foolproof gauge of the seriousness of our acts. A casual perusal of one's own conduct will reveal that we often react much more strongly to relatively minor incidents than to the far more consequential ways we hurt others. We do this through deliberate withdrawal or withholding of affection, for example, or by failing to pay back a loan, or engaging in forms of deception.

THE LACK OF A SIMPLE PROCEDURE OR MECHANISM

One of the reasons the "Oh, that's OK" approach is the socially acceptable method of handling (or rather, *not* handling) personal wrongdoing is that our culture does not have an effective way of addressing such problems. In the absence of a set of gestures and customs that allows people to repent and ask for and receive forgiveness as part of daily life, we conclude, instinctively, that it's better to pretend that it's no big deal, and move on.

Avoidance

Another indirect approach is simply to avoid the person one has wronged. .
- "I told Sue about Jesse's problem and I heard that she told him about what I'd said. I just hope I don't run into Jesse anytime soon."
- "I can't pay Bob back yet for the loan I agreed to repay on the 15th. Maybe if I don't come as usual to 8 o'clock Mass on Sunday, he'll assume I'm sick or something and I'll get another week or two to try to raise the money."

Manipulation

Manipulation involves attempting to win back the favor of the person wronged without actually repenting or asking forgiveness.
- "I've been pretty rotten to my wife lately (work pressures, you know). I'll just send her a surprise gift of flowers and take her to dinner. That should clear things up."

Hiding

Hiding wrongdoing is hoping the other person won't notice.

- "I don't want to make a big deal out of an offhand comment that I'm not sure Pam even heard."
- "Dan is not a sensitive guy. He won't care if I sounded off a little about the behavior of his kids. I was just out of sorts that day. He'll understand."

Waiting It Out

One of the most common forms of evasion we entertain in our society when it comes to wrongdoing is hoping that it will blow over—that if we give the situation enough time, the effects of wrongdoing will evaporate. We imagine that if people don't bring up the problem, this means that it no longer affects or bothers them.

- "It's been a couple of months since I failed to pick up Ann's mother for a medical appointment. After all this time, she can't still hold that against me."
- "Look, don't worry about Bill. He's angry about what you did, sure. But he's an easy-going guy. He'll forget all about it in a week."

Wrongdoing, of course, never really blows over. Unaddressed, it leaves a residue of mistrust and resentment in our relationships, and it also creates a kind of unreal atmosphere in our interactions as we attempt, through indirect comments and humor, to evade the only-too-real effects of our actions. This is the classic theatrical drawing room scene in a domestic drama in which witty, polite, and cheerful conversation masks the deep hurts and misunderstandings that lie just below the surface.

We've all been in parish social halls where the high-spirited banter—if one is listening attentively—barely conceals years of unresolved relational baggage and negative experiences.

The reason all of this is so important is that acts of wrongdoing, whether small or more serious, create hindrances to love. They can not only leave mistrust behind them, but they can also arouse our deepest fears about loving and being loved, about trusting other people and being trustworthy, and cause us to hesitate to take the risks of love that are the heart of Christian life. One of the rationales for dealing quickly and eagerly with repentance and reconciliation has to do with creating an environment of freedom and well-being in our relationships. This makes it possible for us to avoid being enmeshed in a thousand petty squabbles and embrace the Lord's call: To be servants of His love and healing in the world.

The good news is that if we unlearn the patterns of avoidance and evasion and learn to forgive one another and repair wrongdoing as part of daily life, God's grace is there to restore our relationships and make them even better than they were before. If we approach dealing with wrongdoing in the right way, our relationships can be improved precisely in the situations where they've been compromised or hurt. As Paul says about the Law in Romans 6:

Where sin increased, grace abounded all the more. (Romans 6:20)*

This is the promise of reconciliation—not simply that relationships can be more or less restored, or that we can take up where we left off, but that they can be healed and transformed in the very areas where damage had been done. In this way, through taking responsibility for our actions, we become instruments of God's grace in each other's lives—instruments of freedom and transformation.

A Procedure for Repairing Wrongdoing

We've spent a good deal of time discussing attitudes about repairing wrong-doing. But, in the end, as I noted earlier in the chapter, if we don't have a simple method or procedure for addressing the everyday problems that crop up in relationships, we won't be able to handle this area effectively. What I am offering here is a basic four-step approach we have employed for decades in City of the Lord—an approach that many other communities also use. It has the virtue of being simple and practical and when applied with sensitivity and wisdom, has proved over time to help people in the circumstances of daily life to deal with wrongdoing.

In outlining our approach, I'm not implying that there may not be other and better ways of tackling the problem of repairing relationships. But what I would say is that no group or community or parish prayer group or family that hopes to thrive can ignore the need to establish some such method or practice by which members can heal the wounds of daily life and human interaction, and that it must include the basic elements sketched out here.

Simplicity is the key to the method. If the procedure is complicated or cumbersome or involves the need for extensive personal sharing or counseling, life, in my experience, will soon resemble group therapy with predictable results. Everyone will get discouraged and lose heart. While counseling has its place, and serious problems in relationships may require outside or professional help, the point of the procedure is not to encourage speculation about motivations or personal history, or require evaluation of one's emotional state. Amid the rough and tumble of daily life, people must be enabled to take responsibility for their actions and to seek and receive forgiveness.

One preliminary observation: It won't do us much good to talk about repairing wrongdoing if we're not, as individuals and as a body, committed to becoming a righteous and holy people.

But you are a chosen race, a royal priesthood, a holy nation, God's own people, that you may declare the wonderful deeds of him who called you out of darkness into his marvelous light. Once you were no people but now you are God's people; once you had not received mercy but now you have received mercy. (I Peter 2:9-10)

I appeal to you, brethren, by the mercies of God, to present your bodies [your lives] as a living sacrifice, holy and acceptable to God, which is your spiritual worship. Do not be conformed to this world but be transformed by the renewal of your mind, that you may prove [measure] what is the will of God, what is good and acceptable and perfect. (Romans 12:1-2)

And as the *Catechism*, quoting Vatican II's *Lumen Gentium*, states unequivocally:

"All Christians in any state or walk of life are called to the fullness of Christian life and to the perfection of charity." All are called to holiness. (*Catechism of the Catholic Church:* 2013)

This is the essential foundation of all the efforts we're proposing here: our personal and communal response to the God who invites us into His life, and who calls us to be holy as He is holy—to be transformed in mind, heart, and body by His grace—to learn the redeeming culture of the kingdom. No methodology will do much for us if we're not fundamentally committed to becoming, step by step, day by day, faculty by faculty, God's own people—so that our way of life might model His saving love to the world.

Step 1: Honesty

Repentance begins with honesty—admitting wrongdoing, and taking and acknowledging personal responsibility for our behavior. It's worth noting here that we're referring to wrongdoing—to *acts* that are objectively wrong. Temptations, passing thoughts, and emotions are not wrongdoing unless they are acted upon. (Believe me, things can get complicated when over-scrupulous people go around asking forgiveness for their temptations.)

When a Christian realizes or discerns that he has committed wrongdoing in a particular instance—that he or she has acted contrary to Christian standards of conduct—a Christian should acknowledge it simply and directly to God, without introducing issues of blame or extenuating circumstances.

- "It's wrong of me to come home from work and disappear immediately into a video game, ignoring the needs of my family." *Period.*
- "It's wrong of me to take out my personal frustrations on the members of my choir." *Period.*

The behavior of others may, indeed, have contributed to or provoked an act of wrongdoing and our conduct nearly always has a back story, but the point here is that while one cannot take responsibility for others' actions, he or she can and must take responsibility for his own. For a person to repent and be reconciled, he or she must believe that one is personally responsible for one's conduct. It's always helpful in this area to ask the right questions:

ASK:
Was my behavior objectively wrong?
NOT:
"It may have been wrong, but don't you think what she did was wrong, too?"
NOT:
"I admit what I did wasn't the best thing in the world. But am I the only one at fault here?"
NOT:
"Well, I know it isn't right to ignore my family when I get home from work, but, you just don't understand. I'm under a lot of pressure at work and I find it hard to engage in casual chitchat as soon as I get home. Besides, my father treated my mother the same way. Is it my fault if I picked up their bad habits?"

You'll never get a right answer to a wrong question. We need to take personal responsibility for our own actions—regardless of whether we're to blame or not, or whether we think we have an excuse. It's God's job to judge the situation. It's my job to assume responsibility for my own conduct.

Another difficulty in the area of honesty is the temptation to soften the blow through the use of indirect or euphemistic language:

110

SAY:

"I lost my temper with John today."

NOT:

"I was a little aggressive in the way I approached John after the meeting."

SAY:

"I lied to Bob when I told him that Earl had approved the project."

NOT:

"The impression I gave Bob about the status of the project was perhaps a little optimistic."

Blunt is best. This is a deep truth.

I remember going to a particularly good and probing confessor some years ago who, when I confessed a smokescreen of excuses instead of a sin, responded simply, "OK, try again, and this time, tell me what you *did*?"

Honesty is the foundation of repentance and reconciliation. We gain nothing by trying to shield ourselves from the truth of our actions. **The grace of God does not empower our evasions, but our embrace of the truth**—however difficult.

Step 2: Renunciation

The second step in repentance is renunciation—identifying the act, pattern, or attitude as wrong and committing ourselves to change in the area. It is not enough simply to repent personally in the depth of our hearts. We must also commit ourselves to take that course of concrete action that will specifically address the wrong and improve the situation.

Renunciation should be open, verbal, specific, and direct.

- "I harmed Kevin by making jokes about his stutter. This is wrong and I will never joke this way with Kevin again."
- "It was wrong of me to call Sue names just because we disagree about a political issue. This is not the first time I've flown off the handle in this way. I must either learn to manage debate-type situations better, or withdraw from such discussions until I can control my temper."

Sometimes it is easier to admit wrongdoing than it is to renounce it—to make a firm decision to change our behavior in the future. Hard enough under the best of circumstances, renunciation is complicated by the fact that we sometimes like the things we're doing that are objectively wrong.

We can take a certain perverse pleasure from being depressed and from the attention it attracts. We can enjoy being resentful and angry and the sense

111

of power and control over others it brings. We can enjoy the image of ourselves as the great tease, the joker, the one whose sharp wit makes people squirm.

Recognizing the hurtful effects of such common, though sinful, patterns is a crucial part of renunciation.

Another sometimes-neglected aspect of renunciation—although one very familiar to older Catholics like myself—has to do with avoiding the near-occasion of sin. This involves taking decisive steps to avoid placing ourselves in situations, or exposing ourselves to influences that may lead to wrongdoing.

- If Bill finds that he frequently gets out of hand and makes cruel jokes when he drinks a few beers, Bill needs to examine the role of alcohol in his life.
- If a married man finds that counseling young single women causes an increase in sexual temptation, he may need to reconsider the advisability of such co-ed counseling arrangements.
- If Sarah finds herself struggling with anger management issues, it's probably not a good idea for her to see the new movie just out about the notorious tirades of a verbally abusive couple.

Taking steps to avoid occasions of wrongdoing is one of the signs that renunciation is genuine.

A Word about Sorrow

Sorrow for wrongdoing should accompany renunciation. In fact, it's one of the elements that makes the most difference in effecting change in our behavior. Christian, or godly sorrow is a great spiritual boon and should be the focus of earnest prayer as we seek the grace of repentance. This is what classic Christian writers call "the gift of tears."

This authentic sorrow is a far cry from the self-condemnation many people associate with the word. Self-condemnation is a false sorrow that entangles people in self-pity, self-hatred, and despair—and, significantly, remains focused on the self, rather than on God or the person or persons hurt by our actions.

- "You have harmed your family. Once more, you have failed. You're such a worthless person."

Following the voice of this deceptive sorrow leads in only one direction: paralysis, withdrawal, and further hardening of heart. The point is not to wallow in guilt and self-condemnation. The point is to change the way you behave.

Authentic sorrow for wrongdoing is focused on the person injured, the person we have harmed, and on the Lord, whose call to love we have failed to heed. Over time, such sorrow yields insights into the nature of the harm we have caused, and of the attitudes behind them, along with developing compassion for those affected and greater understanding of their sensitivities and needs. As I've noted earlier, true repentance often results, paradoxically, in strengthening our relationships with those we've hurt as well as expanding our own ability to understand ourselves and empathize with others. It also intensifies and deepens our resolution to avoid inflicting such harm in the future and to seek the freedom from sin to which God's grace and our own deepest desires impel us.

Step 3: Reconciliation

The two steps of repentance principally concern our own internal processes—taking responsibility in our minds and hearts for our actions, asking God's forgiveness, and making a decisive personal break with sin and sinful patterns. The next two steps concern others—the process of reconciliation in which we seek forgiveness from those wronged and make restitution, if necessary, for our actions. For obvious reasons, this is often the most difficult part of the process. Life affords abundant proof of the life and healing that asking for forgiveness can bring to relationships, but that doesn't mean that it is ever easy to do.

Asking for Forgiveness

The first question we face is how to ask for forgiveness. How do I ask for forgiveness in a way that leads to a genuine reconciliation? As with renunciation, asking for forgiveness should be open, verbal, specific, and direct.

Forgiveness is not about *if*—if I have offended you—but *in what*. It's about identifying and asking pardon for a specific act of wrongdoing that you've committed, and it's about approaching the person directly that you've wronged.

When asking for forgiveness, there are three things to say to the person you've offended:

1. What I did [specify the wrongdoing] was wrong.
2. I will stop behaving (or relating to you) in this way.
3. Will you forgive me?

We need to acknowledge to the injured party—that is, say it out loud—that what we did to them was wrong and that we intend to change.

- "It was wrong of me to lose my temper like that. I don't want to do that to you. Will you forgive me?"
- "Refusing to greet you when I came home was wrong. I really want to change that pattern. Will you forgive me?"
- "I made jokes about your being out of work. That's wrong. I won't do it again. Please forgive me."

I realize that this formula can have a somewhat artificial or ritual feel to it. As we get used to it and grow in a life of repentance and reconciliation, we may find ways to be a little freer and more flexible with this method or with the wording. However the request is worded, it's essential—for the effectiveness of the reconciliation—that these three elements be present:

- Acknowledgment of wrongdoing
- A resolution to change
- Asking for forgiveness

One of the reasons it's important to insist on a specific approach is the need to counter the confusions and ambiguities—and, hence, the ineffectiveness—of our society's customary ways of handling expressions of regret and repentance. The ordinary way people tend to express regret for wrong actions goes something like this:

- "I'm really sorry about the bad mood I was in yesterday. I had a hard day at work."
- "I feel bad about the way I spoke to you this morning. I had this test on my mind."

Saying, "I'm sorry," doesn't cut it. "Sorry," doesn't take personal responsibility for one's actions. "Sorry," doesn't acknowledge wrongdoing directly. "Sorry," doesn't promise to stop behaving in a wrongful way.

God doesn't require us to feel a certain way about wrongdoing—such as, sorry. He asks us to admit sinful acts and seek reconciliation.

Using the word *apology* can also be a source of confusion.

- "I apologize for what I did."
- "Please accept my apologies for ____."

Apology is a perfectly good word and should be used in the appropriate circumstances. In our community, we tend to use *apology* to refer to instances where someone is hurt or harmed through circumstances that were not under one's control.

It's appropriate (and necessary) to apologize for tardiness when delayed by unexpected traffic. But asking for forgiveness, not apologizing, is in order when the harm is your fault—when, for example, negligence or procrastination led to the late arrival.

There's no doubt that asking for forgiveness is daunting. It's really hard sometimes just to get the words out: "Will you forgive me?" There's a natural and normal resistance that rises in us when we have to ask others for pardon—a resistance born of pride and guilt, to be sure, but also fear of humiliation or rejection. We experience the sheer discomfort of being vulnerable and open to others. A Christian's commitment to love and his or her desire to live in the free-dom of the kingdom must master such fears. Far from an indication that asking for forgiveness is an excessive demand, the emotional turmoil we often feel in the midst of reconciliation is a sign that forgiveness and the power of God's healing love is precisely what's needed. Here are a couple of caveats to think about before asking for forgiveness:

1. In asking for forgiveness, we should ask forgiveness for sinful acts, not, generally, for bad feelings or thoughts that we have toward another person. Avoid saying things like:
    – "I want to ask your forgiveness, Steve, for the resentments I've been harboring against you for months."
    – "I have a bad attitude about you, Joan. I thought you should know."
    – "I need to confess the hostile feelings I've had toward you for the past five years."

    I've actually had people come to me—with the best intentions—and say such things. The result of such confessions is not usually reconciliation and an improvement in the relationship, but an increase in tension and a kind of wariness. One tends to walk on eggshells in the wake of such revelations, wondering just how one might help someone else control their hostile feel-ings toward you or whether others harbor similar feelings.

    If one has allowed negative emotions and attitudes about others to take hold in one's heart, one should repent before the Lord and ask His help to replace those judgments and resentments with His love. But, in general, you should ask for forgiveness only for concrete acts of wrongdoing, not

115

thoughts, temptations, or bad attitudes.

2. One should also avoid turning requests for forgiveness into an opera—overloading the process with extraneous emotionalism or wordiness. Simple and direct is the approach that is required—concise statements that are clear and full of trust in God and others and in the power of forgiveness.

SAY:
   – "What I did was wrong. I want to stop behaving this way. Will you forgive me?"
NOT:
   – "I am so very, very sorry for having done this truly terrible thing. I can't imagine how I could ever have done it! And to you, of all people! I promise you that I shall never, ever do such a dreadful thing again in my whole life. Please, please say that you'll forgive me."

Needless to say, the sentiment communicated by such an appeal is not trust, but fear and anxiety—with a touch of manipulation thrown in for good measure. Keep it simple. The person seeking reconciliation should ask for forgiveness in an honest, clear, calm, trusting and concise way.

Granting Forgiveness

Granting forgiveness in a simple, direct, and decisive way is an equally vital part of this process. **"I forgive you" will do nicely.** Ifs, ands, and buts, in fact, dramatics of any kind, only complicate admissions of wrongdoing and obscure what is needed. It is the life-giving gift of forgiveness, given to others as simply and as abundantly as Jesus grants it to us.

SAY:
   "I forgive you."
NOT:
   "I forgive you, but I won't if this ever happens again."
NOT:
   "I forgive you—but I can't tell you what an idiot you are sometimes."
NOT:
   "I forgive you, I suppose, but I just want you to know that you've hurt me more than I can say. I don't know if I'll ever *really* get over it."

Your brother or sister has asked you simply and directly for forgiveness.

Your response is to grant forgiveness in the same spirit. **A person will ask forgiveness more readily and freely when he or she knows that the injured person will respond with love and acceptance. If you wish to be forgiven freely, freely forgive.**

Here, too, inbred cultural responses may have to be overcome. It's almost automatic for Americans to respond to confessions of wrongdoing with, "Oh, it's OK."

Wrongdoing is not OK. Someone has had the courage to admit wrongdoing and to seek reconciliation. Dismissing the request with a casual indication that they needn't have bothered is a hindrance to the process and, more importantly, to the Lord's work of healing.

Often, "that's OK" means the person being asked to forgive thinks that the incident in question is not that big a deal. This brings us back to the myth of invulnerability problem and to the primacy of emotions.

– "I don't feel all that bad about what you did—how important could it be? Just forget it."

More often, people are simply embarrassed to be in the position of having to forgive someone—to say the words, "I forgive you." This is understandable. But if brothers and sisters who have recognized wrongdoing have to overcome the embarrassment of admitting wrong conduct and ask for forgiveness, you can (and must) overcome the embarrassment of forgiving them.

Ultimately, we forgive one another because of Jesus—and it is Jesus who is working through our forgiveness to unbind the person who has injured us, and to free us from resentment and enmity.

It is good to note in this connection that, as a spiritual writer has wisely remarked, "To forgive is to set a prisoner free and to discover that the prisoner was you."

But it's not only cultural obstacles that can block forgiveness; psychological factors can also play a role.

We may be reluctant to grant forgiveness because we enjoy the sense of being right. To forgive the person who wronged us would mean giving up the feeling of superiority. Forgiving a brother or sister for the wrongdoing they've committed against us may remove the sympathy we've drawn from others by talking about the terrible way we've been treated.

Over time, we can become so comfortable with our resentments that we internalize them, making them part of our identity, part of who we are. Forgiving those who have wronged us threatens our image of ourselves as victims.

While such obstacles can be overcome in the practical realm through the simple act of granting forgiveness, their deeper psychological ramifications—the cleansing of the residue of resentment—often requires earnest prayer—especially prayer before the Blessed Sacrament—and the prayerful support of close brothers and sisters in the Lord.

There may well be additional steps that have to be taken in order to address all the issues that affect particular relationships: professional counseling, further help from wise brothers and sisters, setting specific goals for behavioral reform, recourse to the sacrament of Penance and Reconciliation. And, of course, there's the ongoing struggle with our inner impulses, ingrained attitudes, and thought life—with the condition of our hearts. As admitting wrongdoing is often just the beginning of a process of dealing with sinful patterns in our lives, so **granting forgiveness is not only an act, but the start of a journey to full reconciliation**: a journey that involves the healing of our memories, the cleansing of our minds, and the expansion of our hearts.

But the simple, consistent offering of forgiveness for the wrongdoings of daily life can bring about profound healing in Christian relationships and promote an environment of spiritual health and freedom in the community.

Step 4: Restitution

This final step in the process involves restitution, or making up for acts of wrongdoing when and where it's appropriate. Such a step is essential in cases of wrongdoing where one person has gained something at the expense of another.

If you failed to repay a loan, reconciliation involves not only admitting wrongdoing and asking for forgiveness; it also involves repaying the money. If one admits having stolen, or lost, or damaged an item that belongs to someone else, in addition to asking for forgiveness, one must also return or compensate the owner for the item. This is simple justice. If the one who committed the wrongdoing in such cases does not make restitution, then the genuineness of the repentance is in question.

Someone who has damaged another's reputation through gossip, slander or detraction may need to go to the people that he or she spoke to and unsay them. (Obviously, in such cases, wisdom and care must be taken in doing this.)

A husband who berated his wife in public, after seeking and receiving forgiveness for his wrongdoing, may wish to praise her publicly—not as a way to earn her forgiveness (that, presumably, has already been given), but as a rebuke to his earlier behavior, as an indication that he genuinely recognizes his wife's virtues, and as a sign of a change of attitude.

Living with Christians means living with sinners. Despite our best attempts, we will continue to act wrongly as God continues to work in our lives. Old habits will continue to war with the new life we are given. The flesh—the old man in us—will continue to battle with the Spirit. Patterns of rivalry, envy, judgment, and enmity will continue to mark our journey as brothers and sisters toward the kingdom. In this struggle, God provides us with instruments of grace—sacraments, prayer, fasting, standards of behavior, practical wisdom—that help us handle conflict, address wrongdoing, and bring God's peace, order, and healing to relationships. This simple four-step process of repairing relationships is one of the tools we use in our community life to see that the sun does not go down on our anger (Ephesians 4:26)—to quickly and eagerly repent of wrongdoing and forgive one another, as God in Christ has forgiven us, and to claim for ourselves at the close of each and every day the peace and freedom of the children of God.

Things to Think and Pray About

Dealing quickly and eagerly with repentance and reconciliation in a simple, straightforward way creates a relational environment of freedom and healing. The Holy Spirit wishes to liberate us from a preoccupation with wounds and mistrust, and from the effects of wrongdoing so that we can serve as Christ's ambassadors of reconciliation (2 Corinthians 5:20) in our families and parishes.

- Asking for and giving forgiveness require decisions on our part, but the grace of reconciliation is from the Lord Himself. The reconciliation we administer to one another is the work of His healing and redeeming love.
- "Be angry but do not sin. Do not let the sun go down on your anger." (Ephesians 4:26). Let us claim at the close of each and every day the peace and freedom of the children of God.
- Unacknowledged wrongdoing not only results in mistrust and suspicion, but it arouses our deepest fears about loving and being loved, causing us to hesitate to take the risks of love.

➡ "The reward [of love] is in the joy of loving itself." (S. Schimmel)

➡ "To forgive is to set a prisoner free, and to discover that the prisoner was you." (attributed to Lewis B. Smedes)

119

Chapter 8
Celebration and Family

"As for me and my household, we will serve the Lord."

Joshua 24:15

The family is the privileged place for the transmission of the faith, and it is also a school of prayer...The family, in fact, is an ecclesiola [little church], the first place for evangelization, the domestic sanctuary, where the family prays together...Through the joyous witness of prayer and Christian life, the family becomes the spiritual leaven for the Christian communities... Sunday, the Lord's Day, is characterized by a fruitful and effective remembrance of God's saving acts. The Word of God cannot be absent in family life. Coming together around the Word of life thus becomes a privileged occasion where the family, the domestic church, finds itself fully in the Liturgy of the Christian community.

Jubilee of Families, October 11–13, 2000

Family is the heart of culture. Family is also the heart of the Church, and the school of life and the virtues to which the Gospel leads us. Building Christian brotherhood and sisterhood radiates out from the family.

As St. John Chrysostom, the great fourth-century Church Father, famously put it: the family is the *ecclesiola*, or little church. Summarizing Chrysostom's teaching on the Christian family, Z. Bara writes:

[For Chrysostom], the Church is dependent on the family and the family on the Church; thus they mutually complete each other in this process. The layman's mission is to turn his family into a small church, a cell of the great Church, that is, into a family-church. The core of the Christian community is the Christian family."

This perspective is echoed in the *Catechism* and in the vision of Vatican II:

"The Christian family constitutes a specific revelation and realization of ecclesial communion, and for this reason it can and should be called a domestic church." It is a community of faith, hope, and charity; it as-

120

sumes singular importance in the Church, as is evident in the New Testament. (*Catechism of the Catholic Church:* 2204)

Family Is the Heart of a Spiritual Culture

One of the reasons Christianity, as a whole, is in something of a crisis today has to do with the cultural eclipse of the family and family-centered life. The family, throughout history, has functioned as the privileged place for the transmission of the faith. If the family falls apart or becomes, in cultural terms, a mere shadow of itself, the Church will face daunting internal weaknesses as well as the external challenges those weaknesses invite. As we noted in the chapter on spiritual culture, this eclipse, so evident in the social trends of our day, manages, for the most part, to fly under the radar of much current Christian analysis and strategy. These emphasize program and activity-based solutions rather than organic ones.

Few, I think, will dispute that American family life over the past half-century is in crisis. As family scholar David Popenoe has persuasively argued:

The abrupt and rapid change in the situation of families and children that began in the 1960s caught most family scholars by surprise. At first, there was a great reluctance to admit that a dramatic change was underway. But, although they may differ about its meaning and social consequences, scholars of all ideological persuasions now view the change as momentous and profound....

This period has witnessed an unprecedented decline of the family as a social institution. *Families have lost functions, social power and authority over their members. They have grown smaller in size, less stable, and shorter in life span. People have become less willing to invest time, money and energy in family life, turning instead to investments in themselves.**

If the family is the heart of Christian culture, if the Church itself is a family of families, then one of the essential aspects of building Christian brotherhood and sisterhood in our world is to restore families and family life—to reinvest in the family. A major part of this process has to do with restoring the traditional functions of the family—particularly the family as the center of life, culture, piety, training and education, and the cultural transmission of Christian life. Obviously, this is a large and daunting, and I might add, multi-generational task. But if ef-

121

forts aren't made to effectively restore and refresh family life, then in my experience, efforts to build community will ultimately fall short.

Paradoxically, attempts to build brotherhood and sisterhood in the Lord that do not have as a central aim, the health and vitality of the families involved, often end up as a whirl of activities. Though intended to be supportive, instead they wear everyone out. Even in our community life, where family has always been seen as central, we have periodically had to pull back from or reassess support group and ministry programs. In an attempt to support people, we had overloaded their schedules with activities, thereby taking them away from the very family life community was supposed to foster.

The Biblical Vision of the Home

Given that our culture depicts a truncated sense of what family is and can be, it's useful to reflect on a biblical vision of the home.

Family and the Great Commandment

Hear, O Israel, the Lord your God is one Lord; and you shall love the Lord your God with all your heart, and with all your soul, and with all your might. And these words which I command you this day shall be upon your heart; and you shall teach them diligently to your children, and shall talk of them when you sit in your house, and when you walk by the way, and when you lie down, and when you rise. *And you shall bind them as a sign on your hand, and they shall be as frontlets between your eyes. And you shall write them on the doorposts of your house and on your gates.* (Deuteronomy 6:4-9)*

In considering this passage, we have come full circle. We began our reflections on building a spiritual culture with a chapter on the great commandment, on the primacy of love. Here, in this passage from Deuteronomy—a book that repeats or summarizes the Law, the way of life God wishes to teach His people—we see that the call to love God and neighbor is first of all placed in the context of the family. The very first place where the love of God is taught, learned, and lived is in the family.

The Transmission of Spiritual Culture Is Personal

Notice that this transmission is personal, not professional. Fathers and mothers teach their children directly, imparting to them their own lived experience of faith. This is not a matter of farming out the responsibility to religious ed professionals or easing one's conscience by hoping that attending church will take care of it. Faith is not transmitted by osmosis but in the context of real and committed personal relationships. Obviously, religious education in parishes plays a vital role in the religious formation of children, but it is a supplementary role meant to bolster, confirm, and enrich what is being imparted in the bosom of the family.

It's also worth observing that the form religious education takes in the Book of Deuteronomy is personal and cultural. The passage doesn't imagine that religious formation of children is going to take the form of weekly catechetical seminars conducted by parents around the dining room table. What it does imagine is that parents personally teach and model for their children the life of the virtues, the ways of God, the demands of love, Christian ethics, right speech, honor, gratitude, fidelity and forgiveness. Parents model a whole approach to life, the very spiritual culture we've been outlining in these chapters. And this, again, not based on a syllabus of talks, but on the very way of life, the values the parents themselves live in real time, in the everyday.

And you shall teach [the commandments—God's way of life] diligently to your children, and you shall talk of them when you sit in your house, and when you walk by the way, and when you lie down, and when you rise. (Deuteronomy 6:7)

Deuteronomy envisions parents imparting the love of God and neighbor to their children in the midst of normal activities of family life.

A quotation from a book on the family life of Orthodox Jews may be instructive here. The writer is interviewing a young newly engaged man about his father's influence on his life:

"My father was a man whose main object in life was that he himself [should not do] wrong…that God should be good to him, that he should be able to worship by learning his Torah and by observing his [commandments]. This is one thing. And there is one other main thing, that he should be able to bring up his children in the right way. This I can swear, that if somebody would ask him what you prefer, to make a nice living to be able to give your family all their needs, or to have children and not to be able to make a living, to be poor, but you should have children who follow the Torah and the commandments, I'm quite sure he would choose the second way. *Looking upon him, the way he conducted* *himself and the way he conducted the whole house, I mean, this itself showed what's important in life and how to be."**

This quotation inspires another little aside. It's not unknown in Catholic families for fathers to take the position that religion is the province of women—that their wives will take care of the religious training of children, and that they can safely disappear behind the sports page. Nothing could be further from the truth. Fathers play an essential role in establishing the tone and direction of family life. The vision of the Christian family we are outlining here is not possible unless both parents invest themselves fully in building it.

The other aspect of the religious formation this passage from Deuteronomy envisions has to do with the character of family culture.

And you shall bind them [the commandments] as a sign upon your hand, and they shall be as frontlets between your eyes. And you shall write them on the doorposts of your house and on your gates. (Deuteronomy 6:8-9)

Here the passage refers to the Jewish custom of phylacteries and the *mezuzah* whereby passages of Scripture are attached to devotional objects used in prayer and to the doorposts of houses. The point I'm emphasizing is that the faith passed on in families is not merely a matter of words and concepts, but also of culture, of faith expressed in traditions that engage, inform, and enrich the whole person—mind, body, soul, senses.

This culture involves habits, customs, routines, practices, commitments—even the physical layout of the home itself, as Deuteronomy, with its tokens of faith on doors and gates reminds us. Here I recall the practice of some Eastern Catholics who reserve a corner of the living room—the first room that guests enter—as a holy corner where icons of Christ establish who is the Lord of this home.

Restoring the family as a center of religious culture and tradition—as a place not only of teaching and training, but also of prayer and celebration—is one of the most vital tasks facing us today. As the *Catechism* reminds us:

The Christian family is the first place of education in prayer. Based on the sacrament of marriage, the family is the domestic church where God's children learn to pray "as the Church" and to persevere in prayer. For young children, in particular, daily family prayer is the first witness of the Church's living memory as awakened patiently by the Holy Spirit.

(*Catechism of the Catholic Church:* 2685)

Many older Catholics can still remember festive family celebrations on the major feasts, and on the saint's days of children, weekly family rosaries, prayer before and after meals, and the regular use of sacramentals, such as holy water, in the home. Don't get me wrong. This is not a plea for nostalgia or merely for a return to what we imagine was a simpler past. But it is a recognition that establishing family traditions of prayer, piety, and celebration constitute an essential element in passing on the faith from generation to generation and in the restoration of the full reality of the Christian family itself. The fact that many Catholics, even regular churchgoers, no longer have the experience of a domestic religious culture, who, in effect, live in largely secularized home environments seven days a week, may account for the lack of vitality in whole sectors of American Catholic life.

As we said in an earlier chapter, the parish Sunday Eucharist is the place where the faithful are meant to *bring* the vibrant Catholic life they've been living during the week, to celebrate that life, and be nourished and strengthened by the Lord. Weekly attendance at Mass was never meant to provide a convenient substitute for daily Christian living, but to empower it.

Let me add that developing good home traditions for the transmission and celebration of the faith cannot be conceived merely as a holding action—something to hold off or delay the corrosive effects of an increasingly secular society, to manage to preserve an echo of Catholic faith against the powerful tide of religious indifference. On the contrary, the mission of domestic Christian culture is fundamentally positive—on the offensive. Through a lifetime of training, inspiration, and support, it is meant to help empower the young to be even more faithful, more virtuous, and more effective in their Christian witness than their parents have been.

If we're going to do this in our contemporary context, this will mean establishing priorities for the use of social media—indeed, of all media in the home. It will involve the restoration of families sitting around the dinner table together on a regular basis and going to Mass together on Sundays. It will involve, as our community experience has shown, the need for husband and wife to have a date night—an evening or at least a portion of an evening to have an adult conversation and a chance to renew communication as husband and wife. And it will involve a certain fearless trust in God. As a friend once starkly put it: Parents, fear not; you *are* inadequate. Do all that you can; trust God even more.

Tradition Is a Vehicle for Passing on a Spiritual Heritage

If traditions, by their very nature, constitute a vehicle for the passing on of an inheritance, then the task of tradition is to equip each generation to make an advance, to further the goal of Christian life on the basis of the investment their parents have made— to lead it and move it forward.

What's more, developing and passing on family traditions is not only a matter of fostering and anchoring the faith life of family members, but is part and parcel of the broader work of evangelization to which the Church has repeatedly called the Catholic family. (I cannot help but wonder whether the unfulfilled promise—as I see it—of the Vatican Council's bold vision of the lay apostolate has to do with the neglect of the family—its essential nursery and training ground.)

In this context, it's vital to teach children not only the rudiments of the Gospel, but more comprehensively, to love the truth—to love not opinion or the shifting intellectual fashions of the day, but God's truth, His revelation about what is finally important, about the world, human nature, and destiny. "Through the joyous witness of prayer and Christian life, the family becomes the spiritual leaven for the Christian communities." (Jubilee of Families, 2000) Likewise, the *Catechism* states:

> Daily prayer and the reading of the Word of God strengthen it in charity. The Christian family has an evangelizing and missionary task....The family should live in such a way that its members learn to care and take responsibility for the young, the old, the sick, the handicapped, and the poor. (*Catechism of the Catholic Church:* 2205, 2208)

Let me relate a touching story about the evangelizing effects of the vibrant Christian family. One of our related communities was once densely settled in a neighborhood in the San Fernando Valley within blocks of a long-established Mexican barrio. The leaders decided to send one of their young men into the barrio to find out how their neighbors viewed them. He came back with the report that their neighbors referred to the community members as "the good people." They had seen the way that family life was conducted where the community lived, the respect with which brothers and sisters were treated, the care for the elderly and the young, the singing and prayer that came daily from its households, the evident joy, peace, and confidence on the faces of its members. The earnest wish, he told them, of families in the area was to be able to move closer to the community neighborhood, to be near the good people and the life they led.

It's safe to say, no amount of door-to-door evangelizing—still less of committee meetings on the Catholic family—could have produced that result. The spiritual effects of living the Gospel as a way of life are as incalculable as they are mysterious—and powerful.

Celebration

There are a lot of issues that come to the fore when considering the practical steps that need to be taken to build vital Christian family life. There are three things that we particularly need to keep in mind:

1. Our efforts to culturally renew the family are part of the larger work of restoring Christian culture in our world—the practical dimensions of daily Christian life and witness—and this, in a time of rapid change, confusion and social incoherence. (Suffice it to say, there are other dimensions to that restoration than the ones we're featuring here—for example, the family as a center of work, and of what might be called life-training practical skills, money management, hospitality, life management). Again, the task is not merely or even mainly to protect our values, and ourselves, but also to situate ourselves effectively in the modern world—to build the life and create or renew the traditions that allow us to live as we're called to live, and to pass that life on to our children.

    As my wife Carol often says: what you leave *in* your children is far more important than what you leave *to* your children.

2. Cultural and spiritual traditions—patterns of daily prayer, training, culture of honor, celebration,—have to be seen as our servants. They need to be good human traditions. A flexible, experimental attitude is called for. Traditions need to work. Hence, we need to be as ready to evaluate them as we are to adopt them. Does this practice we've been trying out really bring life? Does it produce the right things in us? Is it, in the end, a burden or a help?

    I remember a situation in which eager parents, fervent in their desire to invest in family life, added dozens of new activities to the family's schedule, mandated praying Morning Prayer from the Liturgy of the Hours before school and breakfast each day, and instituted daily family discussions before bedtime—and wore themselves out and their increasingly disgruntled children before long.

3. Take it easy. Build family culture organically and sensibly. Keep it flexible, and start small. Remember, even adding a few activities to the family's al-

ready packed schedule will be challenging enough. Trying to recreate, re-store, or renew the infrastructure of family life—real communication between parents and children, regular meals together, prayer, celebration—will take time. **The most important single element is the character of the life the parents live in the sight of their children and the love of God and neighbor that permeates the home.**

Keeping Holy the Lord's Day

The Lord's day is the original feast day, and it should be proposed to the piety of the faithful and taught to them in such a way that it may become in fact a day of joy and of freedom from work. (Vatican II, *Constitution on the Sacred Liturgy,* V:106)

Just as God "rested on the seventh day from all his work which he had done," human life has a rhythm of work and rest. The institution of the Lord's Day helps everyone to enjoy adequate rest and leisure to cultivate their familial, cultural, social, and religious lives. On Sundays...the faithful are to refrain from engaging in work or activities that hinder the worship owed to God, the joy proper to the Lord's Day, the performance of the works of mercy, and the appropriate relaxation of mind and body....Christians will also sanctify Sunday by devoting time and care to their families and relatives, often difficult to do on other days of the week....Sunday is a time for reflection, silence, cultivation of the mind, and meditation which furthers the growth of the Christian interior life. (*Catechism of the Catholic Church:* 2184–2186)

If you asked a visitor to our community to describe one of its most charac-teristic and striking aspects, nine times out of ten that visitor would cite our Lord's Day celebration. This celebration, called "the Inauguration of the Lord's Day," is an informal family-based service of prayers, blessings, and songs nor-mally conducted around the dinner room table on Saturday evenings, when, according to liturgical time, Sunday, the Lord's Day, officially begins. If I were to recommend one element of the life of City of the Lord as a possible starting point for building Christian culture in the family-- any Christian family -- my dec-ades of experience would lead me to start here.

This custom goes back nearly to our earliest days as a community and is one of the key elements out of which our life developed—and not ours alone. The Lord's Day celebration is a part of the life of many of the communities that emerged from the Catholic charismatic renewal and, in recent years, has been adopted by students and student groups on many Catholic campuses around the country. It's not too much to say that the Lord's Day is one of the aspects of the particular wisdom God has given to us as a community. It is one of His gifts, and which, with its focus on building out from the family, has deeply influenced the way we think about Christian culture.

Interestingly, the revival of Sunday as the Lord's Day, as a focus of the piety of the faithful and as "a day of joy and freedom from work" was one of the goals of Vatican II. It was partially achieved with some of the liturgical reforms, but outside of Sunday Mass attendance, was hardly a factor in the lifestyle of most Catholics. This is one of those prime instances where groups working to build brotherhood and sisterhood in Christ must take the lead. Notions of the Lord's Day as a day of rest and joy will remain largely theoretical unless modeled by real people in real situations. Christian culture, as always, is created by specific groups and, then, with many adaptations and corrections, reaches a broader public.

This is how the Lord's Day first came to our attention. Most of us community veterans first came in contact with the idea from visits to The Word of God community in Ann Arbor, where, early on, they developed a particular approach to setting aside the Lord's Day. Borrowing from Jewish Sabbath tradition, they gathered on the eve of Sunday around the dining room table to sing festive songs, light candles, pass a glass of wine around the table along with the appetizers and sit down to a leisurely supper, with plenty of light-hearted sharing and discussion.

This was their way of trying to set aside the day, to keep Sunday holy, to spend it differently than one spent the other days of the week—to relax the schedule, spend more quality time with community members and family, and to take time to reflect and pray.

Over time other communities, including ours, took up the idea and developed their own versions of the inauguration of the Lord's Day.

I think what impressed me most about those early experiences with the Lord's Day was the joy—the idea that Sunday, for Christians, was to be a day of joy, singing, and celebration, a weekly experience of the reality of the resurrection. For me, I think, the resurrection was more like an article of faith than an experience. Inauguration of the Lord's Day challenged me to put aside the troubles of the week, the stresses of work, and the worries about children, money, and the future that preoccupy most of us and give myself over—even for the day—to tasting the joy of Christ's victory.

In this, of course, the Christian Lord's Day, takes its cue from the Jewish Sabbath:

Remember the Sabbath day, to keep it holy. Six days you shall labor, and do all your work, but the seventh day is a Sabbath to the Lord your God; in it you shall not do any work, you or your son, or your daughter, your manservant or your maidservant, or your cattle, or the sojourner who is within your gates; for in six days the Lord made heaven and earth, the sea, and all that is in them, and rested the seventh day; therefore the Lord blessed the Sabbath day and hallowed it. (Exodus 20:8-11)

The idea here is that because God rested on the seventh day from His work in creation, His people do as well—not only in imitation of God, but also as a participation in His rest. This life-giving rest means completion, a release from the weekday world of striving, effort, and acquisition, an anticipation of the rest of heaven.

I'm reminded here of the Jewish notion that, rich or poor, in times of trouble or peace, on the Sabbath, every man is a king.

I can't (and won't) digress into a discussion of the relationship between Jewish Sabbath and Christian Lord's Day except to note, as the Catechism does, that they are different.

Sunday is expressly distinguished from the Sabbath which it follows chronologically every week; for Christians its ceremonial observance replaces that of the Sabbath. In Christ's Passover, Sunday fulfills the spiritual truth of the Jewish Sabbath and announces man's eternal rest in God. (*Catechism of the Catholic Church:* 2175)

In the course of the early centuries of Christianity, the weekly Sunday gathering of Christians to honor the day of the resurrection gradually adopted the rhythm and spirit of the Jewish Sabbath. But it did so in a new key, celebrating not so much the work of the first creation as that of the new creation inaugurated in the rising of Christ from the dead.

Jesus rose from the dead "on the first day of the week." Because it is the "first day," the day of Christ's Resurrection recalls the first creation. Because it is the "eighth day," following the Sabbath, it symbolizes the new creation ushered in by Christ's resurrection. For Christians, it has

130

become the first of all days, the first of all feasts, the Lord's Day—Sunday. (*Catechism of the Catholic Church:* 2174)

It's worth stressing that whichever Lord's Day traditions we adopt or develop, the overriding purpose of such domestic customs, for Catholics, is to prepare for and enhance the central reality of Sunday, which is the weekly Sunday Eucharist. The Lord's Day ceremonies, in this sense, perform the role, in domestic terms, of the Sunday Liturgy of the Hours, in framing the celebration of the central mystery of the faith. In some of our households, the Scripture readings of the Sunday Mass are read in preparation for the Sunday Liturgy of the Word, or one of the four Gospels of the Resurrection from the Sunday Office of Readings.

As I see it, the Lord's Day is designed to accomplish two practical ends: finding rest in each other and honoring one another.

Finding Rest in Each Other

The Lord's Day is designed to thwart the notion, so common in our culture, that rest, relaxation and recreation are to be found either in solitude—in avoiding social situations and obligations—or in diversions, the social evasions that contemporary media so abundantly provide (films, TV, video games, social media, etc.).

A friend once told me the story of how he came to embrace the Lord's Day. He had been giving an all-day retreat that particular Saturday. As the proceedings wound down, he found himself looking forward with increasing anticipation to the retreat's end and a well-deserved solo drive to the seaside to watch the sunset and a quiet solitary dinner somewhere.

Just as he was executing his escape, an associate reminded him that tonight was the night he, the retreat director, had scheduled the first-ever Lord's Day celebration at his single men's household. People were already there waiting for him.

He greeted this news with understandable frustration and regret. Gone was the promise of a quiet relaxed evening, putting himself together after a long and exhausting day. Instead, there were more duties and social obligations awaiting him. After walking around the block a few times to work off his "attitude," he steeled himself to face his brothers gathered for the Lord's Day at home.

When he arrived, the brothers in his household took his coat, aware of the long day he'd had, and ushered him into his favorite chair. Dinner was already cooking on the stove. The table was set. Someone had taken the trouble to get all the pamphlets for the Lord's Day service in place. The guitarist was tuning up. Everything had been taken care of. He didn't need to supervise or organize anything.

When the time came for the meal to begin, he apologized to his house-mates for his lack of energy. He just didn't feel up to much tonight, he told them.

"But you're home," someone replied. "We knew it would be a hard day for you today. Relax. You're with us. Nobody expects you to perform."

As the evening wore on, he came to a major realization. He had been seeking peace in a quiet evening by himself, in isolation, but had found it in the presence of his brothers. This is the lesson of the Lord's Day. Not that it's never OK to have a quiet dinner by yourself, but that real peace, the Lord's peace, His rest, genuine recreation is found in the midst of loving relationships. The Lord's Day is designed to teach and establish this reality in our lives.

Honoring One Another

Another practical aim of Lord's Day customs is to honor family relationships. It's vital in building brotherhood and sisterhood in Christ to make explicit and external—to turn into culture—the honor and respect we entertain inwardly, the respect we have in our hearts toward those whose commitment and labor sustain us and make our life possible. Expressing honor in the family is also a key way to educate and form children in an appreciation of the gift of their parents and of the specific contributions each member of the family makes to its life and mission.

Expressing honor in a direct, unambiguous way is not easy in our society. We've all been brought up in a culture that finds open expressions of respect embarrassing—to be deflected by a nearly automatic resort to self-deprecating humor. Part of that reflex is due to the culturally inbred sense that honor and praise is necessarily linked to performance rather than to role.

The weekly celebration of the parental role in the family, coupled with recognition of the blessings of children—regardless of whether parents feel that they've been "star athletes" as parents that week, or that children have behaved like angels—is, in fact, crucial. The honor due to parents is not conditioned on perceptions of their success, nor is the honor and respect due to children conditional on their performance as family assets.

The Lord's Day's celebration of the family reaffirms in an unmistakable way the covenantal character of the Christian family, and the unconditional bonds that hold it all together in the mercy, kindness, and love of God.

In this context, the parental blessing of children as part of the normal weekly or even daily routine is important. Honoring family members on birthdays and other occasions of special importance is vital to psychological and spiritual health, and as an example of the family's role as emblem of unconditional love.

The Lord's Day ceremonies that have been developed in covenant communities over the past forty years have almost all tended to highlight the role of women in the family, particularly the work and ministry of mothers. Given the gender-oriented tensions in our society, and the ambivalence our secular culture shows toward the role of women in the family, underscoring the vital importance of the contribution of women is both a corrective to cultural attitudes and a vital and formative witness to the truth.

Borrowing from Jewish tradition, our celebration includes the recitation of Proverbs 31, the hymn to the virtuous wife—a declaration of praise, surely, but also a recognition of women as strong, capable, and gifted partners in the family building enterprise:

A good wife, who can find?
She is far more precious than jewels.
The heart of her husband trusts in her,
And he will have no lack of gain.
She does him good and not harm
All the days of her life....
Strength and dignity are her clothing,
And she laughs at the time to come.
She opens her mouth with wisdom,
And the teachings of kindness are on her tongue.
She looks well to the ways of her household,
And does not eat the bread of idleness.
Her children rise up and call her blessed;
Her husband also, and he praises her:
"Many women have done excellently, but you surpass them all."
Charm is deceitful and beauty is vain,
But a woman who fears the Lord is to be praised.
Give her the fruit of her hands,
And let her works praise her in the [city] gates. (Proverbs 31:10-31)

Here are some additional areas where Catholic families might want to concentrate their attention. As Lord Day's observances highlight and prepare for the Sunday Eucharist, the liturgical seasons provide a natural context for evolving family customs. Advent is particularly rich in this regard. There is the venerable tradition of singing Christmas carols. Many ethnic traditions, such as Posadas, are there for Catholics to tap into, as well as a plentiful literature on other home-based Advent customs. Lent, too, is a golden opportunity for home evangelization and formation. Easter, in my experience, could use some cultural development in the domestic sphere. The season, in terms of home-based customs, tends to get sidetracked into the secular Easter bunny business. Marian feasts offer many opportunities for home-based observances.

A custom we adopted in our family for Christianity's most important single feast—the feast of the Resurrection—involved erecting a small tomb covered with plaster and rocks on the dining room table and guarded by a toy soldier. The body of Jesus was supplied by a corpus from a crucifix. The first child out of bed Easter morning got to take Jesus out of the tomb and light the Easter candle. During Easter week, we placed a picture of the risen Lord next to the tomb.

Scripture, as the Church rightly urges, should be central to family culture. Reading the weekly Mass readings, with perhaps a family discussion over Sunday breakfast, is a fairly easy, uncomplicated way to focus the family's attention on the riches of the liturgical year and facilitate, over time, a broad familiarity with much of Scripture.

Music can also play a role in establishing a special atmosphere around the Lord's Day and other holy days during the year. In our family, we'd always put on sacred music when the family gathered on Sundays.

In addition, many families develop domestic traditions around the all-important Sacraments of Initiation—Baptism, Confirmation, and First Communion. These occasions provide great opportunities for teaching about and discussion of the meaning of the sacraments in our lives and for imparting a sacramental vision of life.

In the end, building family culture and establishing good Christian traditions in our homes is not really about our efforts, but about God's. We are not the ones who establish the way of life or construct the culture; it is God who creates a life for His people.

Developing traditions that impart life across the generations is a spiritual operation; it's a matter of receiving a life from the Lord; it's a matter of allowing the Holy Spirit to bring to concrete expression all that God has for us in the life of the Church.

We are all witnesses to the life that comes with surrender to God and to His will. But the life that God has been teaching and forming in us is only a shadow of the fullness of that Life that will be revealed in the kingdom of heaven.

Therefore, a Sabbath rest still awaits the people of God; for anyone who enters God's rest, rests from his own work as God did from his. Let us then make every effort to enter that rest. (Hebrews 4:9-11)

As the early Christian writer Origen wrote:

The Christian people govern themselves according to the traditions of heaven, as they move ever toward the presence of the living God and His City [the final and ultimate culture], the heavenly Jerusalem.

Things to Think and Pray About

Family is the center and nursery of the spiritual culture of love and support outlined in these chapters. The restoration and enrichment of the Catholic family as the domestic church is one of the crucial tasks of our time. Setting aside the Lord's Day (Sunday) as a family is a good place to start. Let's open our hearts to the vision of the family God wishes to teach us in the power of His Spirit.

- "The family is the privileged place for the transmission of the faith." (Pope John Paul II)
- Building Christian brotherhood and sisterhood radiates out from the family. We are called to reinvest in the family and in family-centered life.
- The most important single element in religious education is the character of the life parents live in the sight of their children and the love of God and neighbor that permeates the home.
- We do not teach by what we say, but by what we are.
    - "The Lord's Day is the original feast day and it should be proposed to the faithful and taught to them in such a way that it may become in fact a day of joy." (Vatican II, *Constitution on the Sacred Liturgy*)
    - The Lord's Day celebration is meant to thwart the notion that rest, relaxation and recreation are to be found only in solitude – in avoiding social interactions -- or in empty diversions.

Conclusion: Part 2—The Building Blocks of Spiritual Culture

In describing these building blocks, I have attempted to lay out a vision of spiritual and moral culture that I truly believe must inform and shape Catholic life in all of its many manifestations. For all its necessary limitations, the patterns I have described in this book—right speech, gratitude, honor, forgiveness, reliability, and celebration (family)—are the non-negotiables of a universal Christian culture.

That the six building blocks are deeply linked should be evident as well. With right speech at the head, gratitude, honor, forgiveness, and reliability could easily be seen as the fuller outline, in a positive sense, of what godly speech should sound like, with family as both its nursery and destination.

It's strange that while we Catholics have left powerful monuments to faith in our historic cathedrals and in the great heritage of sacred music—creations that still stir men and women to faith and prayer—we have been less successful, generally, in establishing the culture of love, the moral culture that the New Testament implies should be our principal witness in the world.

Therefore, my beloved...work out your own salvation with fear and trembling; for God is at work in you, both to will and to work for his good pleasure. Do all things without grumbling or questioning, that you may be blameless and innocent children of God without blemish in the midst of a crooked and perverse generation, among whom you shine as lights in the world, holding fast the word of life. (Philippians 2:12-16)

I chose particularly those elements that I myself found (and find) both most challenging, and which came as something of a revelation to me and my brothers and sisters as we sought to build community. There are many other things that come into play when building Christian personal relationships. But without right speech, gratitude, honor, reliability, forgiveness and celebration—and these appropriated as a way of life—I don't think that Christian love, in a practical, concrete sense, can be much more than a hope.

Part 3

Concluding Thoughts

Chapter 9

Challenges and Caveats

Nothing worth doing is completed in our lifetime; therefore, we must be saved by hope. Nothing true or beautiful or good makes complete sense in any immediate context of history; therefore, we must be saved by faith. Nothing we do, however virtuous, can be accomplished alone; therefore, we are saved by love. No virtuous act is quite as virtuous from the standpoint of our friend or foe as from our own standpoint. Therefore, we must be saved by the final form of love which is forgiveness.

Reinhold Niebuhr (1952)

Over the years, I have had the enriching experience of traveling across the country and around the world visiting Catholic lay associations and sharing insights with dedicated lay leaders from every continent. One of the things I've noticed in these travels is that with all the changes that inevitably take place over the decades, the one enduring feature of community life is the reality and depth of the life lived together as brothers and sisters in Christ.

It's clear to me now, after half a century of doing this, that community, at the fundamental level, really isn't about ideas, or projects, or leaders, or apostolates, or success, for that matter. It's about *these* people who have chosen to make an article of faith real and concrete: to be each other's brothers and sisters in Christ. In addition to whatever else they are doing in the Church and the world, have decided to risk the challenge of covenant love. They are ordinary people who've prayed for and served one another day in and day out, who've been there for each other on the long nights when life and death were in the balance. They've found a way to love people who are not their sort, or who make them suffer, who've learned to be loyal to relationships even when that loyalty requires personal sacrifices. They've laid aside cherished ambitions and dreams and have found deep and lasting joy in the small and imperfect triumphs of others.

As Fr. Henri Nouwen has perceptively written in his book *The Only Necessary Thing*:

Nothing is sweet or easy about community. Community is a fellowship of people who do not hide their joys and sorrows but make them visible to each other in a gesture of hope. In community we say: "Life is full of gains and losses, joys and sorrows, ups and downs—but we do not have to live it alone. We want to drink our cup together and thus celebrate the truth that the wounds of our individual lives, which seem intolerable when lived alone, become sources of healing when we live them as part of a fellowship of mutual care."

Come and See

Nothing stands out so sharply as an enduring grace and as the preeminent mission of Christian life as the witness of being brothers and sisters in the Lord.

As Jesus says to Andrew, when this first-called of the Apostles asks where to find Him, "Come and see." (John 1:39) Designing programs and outreaches is not the challenge for Christian witness to the world—at least not in the first place—but in being able to say to the world, "Come and see." That is, if you wish to see what Christianity looks like, with all its glories and struggles, come and see my family, my parish, my prayer group, my convent. Not that any of our families, parishes, prayer groups, or communities is a perfect, or even adequate witness—far from it. (In fact, as I'll enlarge on later, our principal witness is to our incompleteness and brokenness, that is to say, to a hope placed elsewhere than in ourselves.) The witness encountered in my own community, I can assure you, is decidedly a work in progress, and a messy one at that, but if we can't bring people home, in effect, to see Christian brotherhood and sisterhood in action, then it's difficult to know what we mean by our apostolic endeavors.

Evangelization without the concrete witness of Christian love is one reason why many attempts at renewal have an abstract, theoretical ring to them—lots of programs, little context; lots of doing but precious little being. In the end, we have nothing to sell, not even Jesus; all we can offer is an invitation to a relationship with the God who has decided to pitch His tent among sinners.

As Catholicism has always understood, the individualistic Jesus-and-me approach to evangelization seriously misses the mark. One is evangelized *by* a faith community and *into* a faith community. Insofar as we are striving to grow in the fruit of the Holy Spirit—love, joy, peace, patience, kindness, goodness, faithfulness, and self-control—and in the hope of our confession, people will be drawn to Christ and His Gospel. Despite our manifold and only-too-apparent inadequacies, they'll come and they'll see. As Pope Paul VI writes:

The Church is therefore holy, though having sinners in her midst, because she herself has no other life but the life of grace. If they live her

139

life, her members are sanctified; if they move away from her life, they fall into sins and disorders that prevent the radiation of her sanctity....She has the power to free her children through the blood of Christ and the gift of the Holy Spirit.

Or, as Vatican II states: "Holiness is the hidden source and infallible measure of [the Church's] apostolic activity and missionary zeal."

There is a reason why focusing on living as brothers and sisters in Christ as our essential witness to the life of grace is still, despite the urgings of the New Testament, something of a novel approach. It's hard. I can tell you from experience, no matter how many years you've been at it, trying to live in Christian love, and according to the principles laid out in earlier chapters, it always cuts against the grain of inbred tendencies in us that Scripture calls "the flesh."

> But I say, walk by the Spirit, and do not gratify the desires of the flesh. For the desires of the flesh are against the Spirit, and the desires of the Spirit are against the flesh; these are opposed to each other to prevent you from doing what you would.... Now the works of the flesh are plain: fornication, impurity, licentiousness, idolatry, sorcery, enmity, strife, jealousy, anger, selfishness, dissension, party spirit, envy, drunkenness, carousing, and the like....If we live by the Spirit, let us also walk by the Spirit. (Galatians 5:16-25)

Reestablish Natural and Stable Structures

In addition to the perennial difficulties of walking the walk of the Spirit, there are particular difficulties in trying to build a spiritual culture in today's environment. As I noted above, many of the natural structures that once undergirded and supported practical Christian life have been dismantled—stable neighborhoods, natural support systems for women and men, the home as the center of life. This means that, in many cases, we must recreate elements of these natural structures, such as support systems and family culture, in order to make our brotherhood and sisterhood real, that is, a practical daily reality rather than an ideal. This involves much improvisation and trial and error. And, it's worth noting, many, many mistakes.

A second particular difficulty is the nature of modern culture itself. Much of today's culture is built on the idea of dissolving bonds of connection rather than building or maintaining them—based on a radical ideal of consumerist individualism. (Even the ubiquitous social media which promises to expand interpersonal connections, in fact, merely advertises how abstract our current notions of human connection really are.) Attitudes promoted in popular culture and the media often make it doubly difficult to build Christian relationships in any sort of meaningful way. Part of deciding to be brothers and sisters in Christ in our day involves many difficult decisions to restrict and contain exposure to cultural currents that undermine these values and to build our lives around activities and relationships that support them.

In my experience, this certainly means containing the constant flow of popular media in the modern American home—not only social media, but also video games, television, talk radio, and Internet usage—in favor of direct communication between family members during daily meals, family prayer, quality time for parents and children, personal sharing, and hospitality.

The Danger of Legalism

Another danger inherent in this project is a subtler, but nonetheless potentially destructive one: the danger of legalism. As emphasized throughout this book, these principles for building Christian relationships are the molds into which the Holy Spirit pours His grace. The principles themselves are only the beginning of the process. They are specific behaviors, which over time, in generous hearts and with the power of the Spirit, become relational habits, spiritual instincts—Christian character. In that sense, they're like the manners we try to teach our children. At first, the do's and don'ts are simply rules to be obeyed. Our hope as parents is that these rules eventually become genuine habits and personal qualities—courtesy, kindness, thoughtfulness. In a real way, the tale only gets interesting when principles have disappeared into character, when we act in Christian ways with a naturalness and ease born of experience and the integration of principles with our own individual personalities. This, then, becomes the basis for an even deeper journey from good Christian character to sanctity.

Legalism, on the other hand, is a kind of spiritual disease that stunts this process, stopping far short of the goal in a strict focus on the rules. We all have to start somewhere, of course, but a stern, rigorist approach to developing Christian relationships is a spiritual cul-de-sac. Such an approach—itself a form of spiritual immaturity—will tend to discourage people, with the result that everyone more or less abandons the effort to change. Patience and, above all, charity, constitute the only way forward, along with a steady focus on the grace of the Holy Spirit without which the building of Christian character is not possible. Always keep in mind that principles are merely the beginning of the process.

The focus on rules, perhaps necessary at the outset, can often be a form of evasion, a paralyzing failure to grasp the larger perspective of love and personal surrender to God (see the Parable of the Pharisee and the Publican—Luke 18:9-14).

Inflexibility and the tendency to judgment is one of the telltale signs of the disease of legalism. Life experience teaches us that the changes God wants to produce in our lives come about not in an environment of judgment, intolerance, and rigor, but in one that recognizes how daunting the work before us really is. Much creativity and flexibility is required to respond to God's unfolding plan in our lives. Clarity and tough-mindeness must be informed, even corrected at times, by mercy.

As an old friend and mentor, Fr. Charles Harris, once said at a retreat:

The habit of not judging others is generally the mark of a mature Christian....No one can judge human beings but God, and God is so merciful because He is so wise.

Living with Disagreements

One of the most difficult challenges of building Christian brotherhood and sisterhood is learning to live with disagreement. You will realize at once that you are reading the words of an old man since I did not write "overcoming disagreements," but "*living*" with them. Some disagreements can be resolved through discussion, prayer, good will and humility. But some issues that divide us in the course of the years may not yield easily, despite our best and most conscientious efforts. The question then is: How can we manage disagreements without succumbing to divisiveness, without breaking the bonds of brotherhood?

The essential thing to remember is that disagreements, like the poor, will always be with us. There were serious disagreements even among the Apostles who had personally seen the Risen Christ:

But when Cephas [Peter] came to Antioch, I [Paul] opposed him to his face, because he stood condemned. For before certain men came from James, he ate with the Gentiles, but when they came he drew back and separated himself, fearing the circumcision party. And with him the rest of the Jews acted insincerely, so that even Barnabas was carried away by their insincerity. (Galatians 2:11-13)

However serious the disputes among the Apostles, however, they were still brothers in the faith. It's safe to say that if some of the historic disputes in Christianity had been handled in covenant love, they may well have not resulted in some of the divisions that have plagued Christianity over the centuries.

But handling serious disagreements is a daunting business, and disagreements *will* arise even in the most apparently cohesive and unified groups.

So, these notes about disagreement, far from being theoretical, distill some painful lessons and some costly insights.

Tips for Managing Disagreements

- **Right Speech**

  A commitment to right speech will militate against some of the worst effects of dispute and disagreement. If serious disagreement emerges in a group, ground rules should be established at the outset. For example, how we're going to conduct ourselves as we seek clarity, understanding, and common ground, so that all sides are fairly heard and so that unity and the personal reputations of the disputants can be protected as we do so.

- **Respectful Discussions**

  Having a respectful discussion geared toward understanding the points of view, particularly the background, experiences, and fears of the participants, is essential. Be ready to explore whether language and terminology is part of the problem.

- **Respect**

  Respect is key. Avoid labeling people ("arch-conservative," "muddle-headed," "rebellious")—treat them as brothers and sisters, not as token representatives of a position. Conduct the discussion in truth *and* in love.

- **Patience**

  Be prepared to be **patient** with situations that seem irresolvable. Prayer and fasting reach places with each other that we otherwise cannot reach.

- **Preserve Fellowship**

  Refuse to disfellowship or exclude people, except as a last resort. Sometimes, frustrations with perceived opposition cause us to disfellowship first and ask questions later. Be committed to protecting people's reputations even after a decision to separate, and hope that some future resolution or reconciliation may be possible. Don't burn bridges.

Finally, community, whether in lay associations or in parishes or convents, is not about agreeing with one another about everything. Sometimes the tensions and differences are healthy, each tendency a corrective (even a gift) to the other. Community is about loving one another as brothers and sisters. As Fr. Henri Nouwen writes:

> When we form a Christian community, we come together not because of similar experiences, knowledge, problems, color, or sex, but because we have been called together by the same Lord. Only God enables us to cross the many bridges that separate us; only God allows us to recognize each other as members of the same human family; and only God frees us to pay careful attention to each other. That is why those who are gathered together in community are witnesses to the compassionate Lord. By the way they are able to carry each other's burdens and share each other's joys, they testify to God's presence in our world.

God's Initiative

In contrast to humanity, which, history teaches us, is relatively easy to love precisely because it is an abstraction, choosing to be brothers and sisters in the Lord in the concrete sense is both difficult and salvific. It's how God, in practical terms, works to save us, to make us whole, and to prepare us for the life to come. Nouwen, again:

> The Christian community is...a community which not only creates a sense of belonging, but also a sense of estrangement. In the Christian community we say to each other, "We are together, but we cannot fulfill each other....We help each other, but we also have to remind each other that our destiny is beyond our togetherness." The support of the Christian community is a support in common expectation. This requires a constant criticism of anyone who makes the community into a safe shelter or a cozy clique, and a constant encouragement to look forward to what is to come.

Nouwen's perceptive comments point in the direction of a final uncomfortable, old man's truth—in living the Gospel as a way of life, we are called to acknowledge that the Kingdom of God we seek is not only beyond our efforts, it is beyond our vision. We are, as Bishop Kenneth Untener has wisely written, "prophets of a future [that is] not our own."

Nothing we do is complete. Everything we attempt is partial, given over to the work of other hands, part of a whole we can never see. In this sense, we are all Moses who led his people to the Jordan River into a future he glimpsed only

144

from afar. All we can do is what we're given to do—and even the realization of the aims we most cherish and to which we have given everything, will lie beyond us.

[Our work] may be incomplete, but it is a beginning, a step along the way, an opportunity for the Lord's grace to enter and do the rest. We may never see the end results, but that is the difference between the master builder and the worker. (Bishop Kenneth Untener)

This is the source of the humility that is our greatest strength and our source of wisdom: that the results aren't ours but God's. Despite all the hard work that building brotherhood and sisterhood requires, human effort will never produce community. It is God's initiative from first to last. God's call brings it into being, and God's grace is the source of the life that we share. It is in light of His call that we recognize each other as brothers and sisters on a common journey to the New Jerusalem.

All that we are required to do, in the midst of our fears and inadequacies, is to stay put and be faithful. And to that I say, Amen.

Note: I have tried to emphasize throughout this book that the Christian way of life is a life empowered at every turn by the Holy Spirit. Nothing that I've outlined in the previous chapters is possible without turning to the Holy Spirit for His grace, power, and light. Hence, I wish to add this prayer to the Holy Spirit as the final word of this book.

Come, Holy Spirit, come.

Come like Holy Fire and burn within me.
Come like Holy Wind and cleanse me.
Come like Holy Light and lead me.
Come like Holy Truth and teach me.
Come like Holy Love and enfold me.
Come like Holy Power and anoint me.

Come as Abundant Life and
      open me
      fill me
      convert me
      consecrate me
      until I am wholly Yours.

Come, Holy Spirit, come.

- author unknown

For Further Reading

Dietrich Bonhoeffer, *Life Together*, Harper & Row, 1954

Raniero Cantalamessa, *Life in Christ*, Vineyard Publications, 1997

Raniero Cantalamessa, *Obedience*, St. Paul's Books, 1986

Paul Joseph Cardinal Cordes, *Born of the Spirit*, Greenlawn Press, 1992

Paul Joseph Cardinal Cordes, *Where Are the Helpers?* University of Notre Dame Press, 2010

Francis De Sales, *Introduction to the Devout Life*, Image, 1972

Ignatius of Loyola, *The Spiritual Exercises*, Image, 1964

Thomas a Kempis, *The Imitation of Christ*, Paraclete Press, 2008

Francis Martin, *The Life Changer*, St. Bede Publications, 1998

Jean Vanier, *Community and Growth* (revised edition), Paulist Press, 1989

About the Authors

JIM JONES and his wife Carol were part of the original group at Notre Dame University that received the initial outpouring of the Holy Spirit in the late 1960s. From that momentous event, members of the group went out to bring what became the charismatic renewal to people throughout America and other parts of the world.

When the company that Jim worked for moved its corporate headquarters to Phoenix, Arizona in 1969, Jim, Carol, and their seven children followed along at the company's request. In doing so, they also brought their newfound experience of the Baptism in the Spirit to people throughout the Southwest. Thus began a long journey to build what is now the City of the Lord.

GABRIEL MEYER is one of the founders of City of the Lord, Los Angeles, and helped pioneer the community's outreach in Jerusalem in the mid-1980s. He is also an award-winning foreign correspondent for the *National Catholic Register*, who has lived in and reported from the Middle East, the Balkans, and East Africa. He was especially noted for his coverage of the first Palestinian *intifada* and the Bosnian civil war. His reporter's diary on the Sudanese civil war, *War and Faith in Sudan*, won ForeWord Magazine's Book of the Year Award for essays in 2006. He has published poetry and two novels, most recently, the poetic cycle *A Map of Shadows* for Tebot Bach Press. He has also completed a large-scale "biography" of the Church of the Holy Sepulcher in Jerusalem entitled *The Testimony of Stones*. He currently serves as Executive Director for the Southern California Ecumenical Council.

Jim Jones being greeted by His Holiness Pope John Paul II during the formation of the International Catholic Fraternity in Rome in 1990.